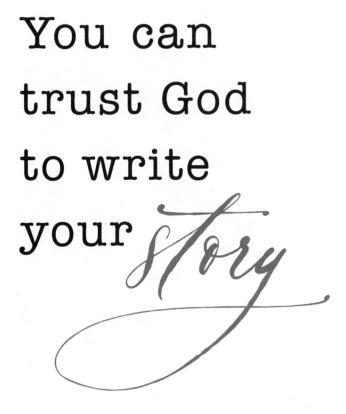

You can trust God to write your *story*

You can trust God to write your *story*

*Embracing
the Mysteries
of Providence*

Nancy DeMoss Wolgemuth
& Robert Wolgemuth

MOODY PUBLISHERS

CHICAGO

Unless otherwise indicated, Scripture quotations are from the ESV® Bible (The Holy Bible, English Standard Version®), copyright © 2001 by Crossway, a publishing ministry of Good News Publishers. Used by permission. All rights reserved.

Scripture quotations marked NASB are taken from the New American Standard Bible®, Copyright © 1960, 1962, 1963, 1968, 1971, 1972, 1973, 1975, 1977, 1995 by The Lockman Foundation. Used by permission. (www.Lockman.org)

Scripture quotations marked NKJV are taken from the New King James Version. Copyright © 1982 by Thomas Nelson. Used by permission. All rights reserved.

Scripture quotations marked NIV are taken from the Holy Bible, New International Version®, NIV®. Copyright © 1973, 1978, 1984, 2011 by Biblica, Inc.™ Used by permission of Zondervan. All rights reserved worldwide. www.zondervan.com. The "NIV" and "New International Version" are trademarks registered in the United States Patent and Trademark Office by Biblica, Inc.™

Scripture quotations marked NLT are taken from the Holy Bible, New Living Translation, copyright © 1996, 2004, 2007, 2013. by permission of Tyndale House Foundation. Used by permission of Tyndale House Publishers, Inc., Carol Stream, Illinois 60188, U.S.A. All rights reserved.

Scripture quotations marked CSB are taken from the Christian Standard Bible.® Copyright © 2017 by Holman Bible Publishers. Used by permission. Christian Standard Bible®, and CSB® are federally registered trademarks of Holman Bible Publishers.

Scripture quotations marked KJV are taken from the King James Version.

Italics in Scripture references indicate author emphasis.

Names and details in some illustrations have been changed to protect individuals' privacy.

Published in association with the literary agency of Wolgemuth & Associates.

Edited by Anne Christian Buchanan
Cover and interior design: Erik M. Peterson
Author photo by Vitaly Manzuk (vitalymanzuk.com).

Library of Congress Cataloging-in-Publication Data

Names: Wolgemuth, Nancy DeMoss, author. | Wolgemuth, Robert D., author.
Title: You can trust God to write your story : embracing the mysteries of
  providence / Nancy DeMoss Wolgemuth and Robert Wolgemuth.
Description: Chicago : Moody Publishers, [2019] | Includes bibliographical
  references. |
Identifiers: LCCN 2019017425 (print) | LCCN 2019020750 (ebook) | ISBN
  9780802498144 () | ISBN 9780802419514
Subjects: LCSH: Providence and government of God--Christianity. | Trust in
  God--Christianity. | Trust in God in the Bible.
Classification: LCC BT135 (ebook) | LCC BT135 .W63 2019 (print) | DDC
  231/.5--dc23
LC record available at https://lccn.loc.gov/2019017425

ISBN: 978-0-8024-1951-4

We hope you enjoy this book from Moody Publishers. Our goal is to provide high-quality, thought-provoking books and products that connect truth to your real needs and challenges. For more information on other books and products written and produced from a biblical perspective, go to www.moodypublishers.com or write to:

Moody Publishers
820 N. LaSalle Boulevard
Chicago, IL 60610

3 5 7 9 10 8 6 4 2

Printed in the United States of America

*T*o Nancy's beloved pastor, Dr. William Hogan,
under whose preaching she was nurtured during her childhood
and teen years. Through his ministry of the Word,
she grew to treasure and trust the sovereignty of God
as a good and precious gift. Bill could not have imagined
how his influence in this young woman's life—
and that of his dear wife, Jane—would someday become
one of God's kindest gifts to me.

Robert

In God's sweet Providence, more than forty years later,
Bill's life became further intertwined in the story God
was writing in Robert's and my lives when he officiated
our wedding. As we turned the page to a new chapter in our
story that day, this faithful servant in his eighties reminded us:

Who goes before you?
The King of glory!

This continues to be our confidence as we wait on the edge
of our seats in anticipation of all that our King has in store
for His followers in the days and ages to come.

Nancy

*All my days were written in your book and planned
before a single one of them began.*

PSALM 139:16 CSB

Contents

Before you begin . . .

*D*uring a recent trip to Maryland, I drove beyond our family farm to visit the campus of Western Maryland College. I wanted to meander the commons and courtyards of this old Methodist college I originally planned to attend. Had much changed since 1967, when I would've been a freshman? As I wheeled past the brick buildings, I kept thinking, *how different my life would've been had I graduated from here.* My goal was to become a physical therapist, but who knows? Maybe I would've changed my major, left school to marry, or even wandered away from my fledgling Christian faith.

All I know is that Jesus had a much better design for my life. I paused on a hill overlooking the athletic field and smiled. Yes, I got into physical therapy . . . but as a quadriplegic from a diving accident just weeks before my college orientation! *Never, ever did I dream I would come to this school as a visitor in a wheelchair.*

And a very contented visitor. I felt no hint of remorse or regret. Not once did I envy the girls on the athletic field, practicing lacrosse. To be honest, I couldn't wait to get back in the van and continue the drive to our Joni and Friends' Family Retreat just north in the Pennsylvania mountains.

God has made His design for my life abundantly clear—for

the past forty years, I have led a Christian ministry that is reaching for Christ hundreds of thousands of disabled people and their families across the US and around the world. We hold retreats for special-needs families across the globe and deliver thousands of wheelchairs to needy kids with disabilities overseas. To give hope and help to hurting people? I can't think of a happier story that God could've written for my life.

And God is heaven-bent on writing satisfying stories in all our lives. You'll discover that in this remarkable book *You Can Trust God to Write Your Story*. God may design some chapters in our lives to be long and delightful; others, far too short, and sometimes painful. But we only see the meaning of our story when it fits into the context of a bigger, far greater story of Jesus Christ Himself. My best life-chapters were not the easy, breezy days of being on my feet; they were the deep ones when I was suffering and groping for the arms of my Savior.

> My best life-chapters were not the easy, breezy days of being on my feet; they were the deep ones when I was suffering and groping for the arms of my Savior.

The authors of this book, Robert Wolgemuth and his wife Nancy, could say the same. I met them both decades ago when Nancy Leigh DeMoss was single and focused on her international teaching ministry. Robert was an executive at Word Publishing, happily married with two children. Their stories seemed easy to read and almost predictable. Anyone could easily guess how God would write their future chapters. But then, the mysteries of God's Providence came into play, forcing them both in uncharted and new directions. Like me, their stories turned out *far* different than originally planned. But that's the glorious part of God's mysterious ways!

So, it's wise to leave our storyline to the best Storyteller of all. If God seems to be writing an unusual story in your life, don't resist His penmanship on the pages of your days. Don't balk against the bumps and bruises He writes into your script. I will be the first to confess that His Providence can, at times, read like a mystery novel, but in the end, His storyline for those who trust Him is *always* wise, specific, and good. Good for you and for others. Best of all, good for the kingdom.

You hold in your hands an amazing book whose title says it all: *You Can Trust God to Write Your Story*. For if you are a follower of Jesus, every day of your life—whether you feel like it or not—is weighted with kingdom purpose, eternal significance, and a royal destiny filled with joy and contentment. Get ready to let my dear friends, Robert and Nancy, help you embrace the mysteries of the Lord's Providence. For when it comes to happy endings, you can't find a better Author than the God of the Bible.

Happy endings are His forte—turn the page, trust Him, and discover it for yourself.

JONI EARECKSON TADA
Joni and Friends International Disability Center

Once Upon a Time

What Makes a Great Story?

> People are looking for stories
> that really mean something—
> stories that are redemptive, inspiring,
> and bigger than an individual.
>
> SCOTT HARRISON

Who doesn't love a good story?

When my (Robert's) daughters were little, I'd sometimes take them with me on Saturday morning to pick something up from Home Depot. And during the drive they'd often say, "Daddy, tell us a story." Their favorites were the ones about them when they were very small and the stories of my own growing-up years.

Of course, stories aren't only for children. Whatever our age, we relish being caught up in a good yarn, whether it's told in person, in a good book, or on a screen. Good stories entertain us; they teach us; they engage our imagination and creativity.

They also connect us with God, the original Storyteller and the ultimate Author of our individual life stories.

This is a book filled with stories. They're all true—though in some cases we've changed names and details to protect people's privacy.

You'll read

- parts of our own stories—some from our growing-up years, others more recent;

- selected scenes from some of our friends' lives, representing various seasons and challenges;

- a few stories of people who lived a long time ago and who continue to inspire us today;

- several accounts of characters found in the Bible, set apart as "interludes" throughout this book. These are real men and women whose lives included unexpected twists and turns and even upheaval at times, just as your journey and ours do.

This is also a book *about* stories. More specifically, it's about the overarching, eternal, often-unseen Story that God is writing in this broken, fallen world. We'll explore what His Story has to do with our individual stories and how it intersects with our unanswered questions and pain.

Before diving into all of that, let's take a moment to rehearse what makes a great story. (Robert: this takes me back to my freshman English class with Miss Kilmer.) For sure, it's more art than science. But behind the beauty and drama of a compelling tale are some essential ingredients. Like unseen two-by-fours inside a wall, they're what make the story stand straight and true.

Let's start with the people in the story . . .

THE CHARACTERS

The Protagonist

Every good story has a protagonist—a character who goes on a journey and is somehow changed. In almost every story, the protagonist is also the main character, the one we focus on from the beginning. And in most stories, the protagonist is also the hero—the one who ends up saving the day. Think the square-jawed Mountie in his scarlet uniform rescuing the damsel in distress or the courageous nurse on the battlefield, dodging mortars and bullets, risking life and limb to save wounded soldiers.

When I was a young boy, weekend television included heroes like Mighty Mouse and Lassie. If this were an audiobook, I'd probably sing, "'Here I come to save the day.' That means that Mighty Mouse is on the way" or I'd whistle Lassie's theme song. These were heroes who captured my imagination as a child. (If you're too young to remember them, you can find them on YouTube!)

The Antagonist

On the other side of the coin is the bad guy. He's the one that makes the audience boo when his image hits the screen . . . or when his name appears on the page. He's the person who gunks up the story. He makes life miserable for the good guy or those he cares about—or even threatens lives.

Everyone loves to hate this guy.

Other Characters

Most stories involve more than two people, of course, so you will also have different characters playing various roles. They may provide help (a sidekick), motivation (a love interest) for the protagonist, or wisdom to guide him or her along the way. They may contribute to complications or plot turns, and in some cases they may act as a witness or narrator for what happens.

And then beyond the people is . . .

THE PLOT

An Inciting Action

We have the players. Now we need an event, a circumstance, a challenge, or a tragedy that sets the characters in motion. This could be a natural disaster or something caused by other people—perhaps the antagonist. "What are they going to do now?" the reader wonders.

A well-conceived story grabs our attention right from the start, giving us a reason to care about the people we've just met. Now something goes wrong, which creates . . .

Conflict

This is where "the plot thickens." A struggle of some sort is introduced to the narrative. Tension builds between the protagonist and the antagonist, and this is what makes the story riveting. Page turning. It's what keeps our attention. The more intense the tension, the less likely it is that we'll be distracted or doze off.

And then all of this comes together so there's some kind of . . .

Climax and Resolution

This is the place in the story where the conflict comes to a head and something is decided. The hero conquers. The villain stumbles and fails. This is what the adventure has built toward from the beginning. The viewer or reader or listener is satisfied with the outcome, and all that remains is to wrap up some details and unanswered questions.

Now, this may not happen quickly. In fact, quite a lot of story may follow the climax. But once we get to the climax of a story, the resolution is just a matter of time.

Not every story, of course, is as simple and straightforward as we have just outlined. In fact, the bigger the story, the more complicated it's likely to be. Sometimes the protagonist and the hero/heroine will be different characters. Heroes may be flawed, and villains may be misguided or confused rather than evil. Side characters may have their own subplots woven in to add interest or texture to the primary story. The action may take unpredictable twists and turns. But all of this typically makes a story even more riveting.

Alex and Stephen Kendrick spend their time looking for and telling great stories. You may have seen some of the films these brothers have produced: *Facing the Giants, Fireproof, Courageous, War Room.* We've watched them all and have shed more than a few tears in the process.

> Situations that seem confusing and chaotic to us are actually plot threads God is weaving together to create a story . . . a beautiful, compelling work of art.

In a conversation about what makes a compelling story, Stephen pointed out that if someone tells a story about a man who, say, gets up, has breakfast, goes to work, comes home, has dinner, and goes to bed, everyone says, "That's boring!" No one likes a dull story. We want it to have intrigue, action, conflict, twists and turns, problems to be solved.

But when it comes down to our lives, we tend to think differently. That "boring," tidy, uncomplicated story—no muss, no fuss—is the way most of us want to live. We want our story and the stories of those we love to have predictable, Hallmark movie endings where everything gets tied up neatly in ninety minutes, the good people fall in love and live happily ever after, and the bad people go away and are never heard from again. So when the unexpected, unwanted twist or turn happens in our own personal life story—when we receive that troubling medical report, open the pink slip, lose the baby, or learn that a friend has been gossiping behind our backs—we may feel disappointed, betrayed, or even devastated.

But God rarely writes neat, tidy, sanitized (boring) stories. In fact, many of the accounts we find in Scripture are pretty messy. The Bible arrests our hearts, changes our lives, and advances His kingdom with stories like Joseph being falsely accused and thrown into prison for refusing the advances of his boss's wife . . . or Daniel being tossed into a lair of lions because he resisted the king's edict outlawing prayer.

Your life and your story actually matter. They have meaning as you view them against the backdrop of God's ultimate Story.

This is no less true in our lives. Situations that seem confusing and chaotic to us are actually plot threads He is weaving together to create a story . . . a beautiful, compelling work of art. Incidents and events that make no sense at all now will one day make perfect sense—if not in this life, then in heaven—as we see the masterpiece He had in mind all along.

The stories found in this book have protagonists, antagonists, actions, and conflicts. Some have resolution, others not yet. But none of them are finished. God is still writing His story in and through each of us.

Our hope is that as you read these accounts you'll be encouraged and inspired to trust Him with *your* story. But here's something else that's important to keep in mind: *each of the stories in this book is part of a bigger, grander, eternal Story God is writing.*

And that's true of your story, too.

This should comfort and encourage you—to know that your life is not just a speck drifting on an ocean of time, lost among the billions of other people who have ever lived. Your life and your story actually matter. They have meaning as you view them against the backdrop of God's ultimate Story.

That grand Story is unlike any other ever written.

$\sim$

"In the beginning"—once upon a time, that is, a long time ago, in fact, before there was such a thing as time or anything else, for that matter—"God . . . " (Gen. 1:1).

This Story opens with God on center stage.

Only God. Apart from Him, nothing. Complete darkness. This is not just a stroll in the country on a moonless night. This is terminal vacancy.

And then a voice. His voice. And for six consecutive days, this voice speaks everything into existence. Mountain ranges and molehills. Stars and sand. Leviathans and lizards. This week of creation—turning nothing into everything—concludes with the forming of a man and a woman.

God's Story continues in a garden.[1] Perfect, pristine beauty. Made for the couple He had created to enjoy unending pleasure and relationship with Himself.

The Protagonist? God Himself. He is the Main Character, the Author, the Hero. This Story is by Him, about Him, and for Him.

Then . . . enter the serpent, the antagonist of all antagonists.

The villain of all villains. His mission is to destroy what God had created, to crush the flawless beauty of the garden (called Eden) and its residents. And the antagonist succeeds in this effort, wreaking havoc not only on the garden and that first couple, but on the entire planet and every human (save One) who would ever set foot on it.

That's the inciting action. And in no time at all, there's conflict. Jealousy between the first two children born to the first parents results in history's first homicide. One brother murders the other and then, like his dad, tries to hide his sin from the Creator.

For the thousands of years that follow, smaller stories unfold inside the grand Narrative. We encounter champions and criminals. Luminaries and losers. Medalists and miscreants.

And then the Protagonist steps into the scene once more. The unseen God who fills heaven and earth becomes visible and is held in a mother's arms. The almighty Creator of all flesh is wrapped in frail flesh. Unto us a Savior is born—the second Adam. And with that birth God's great Story surges toward a climax. This groaning, shackled earth is about to be released from its bondage. History—past, present, and future—is about to be rewritten.

There's a lot more to the story, of course. We are still living in the long resolution of God's great Story, as the plot threads are being tied together and all history is moving toward the final, satisfying ending—that Day when all things will be made new.

No story ever told could compare to God's great Story. None other is as compelling, transforming, or hope-giving.

And your story and our story are part of it.

CHAPTER 1

Of Birds, Flowers, and You

Living under Providence

How unspeakably precious and sweet it is when we
can believe that God our Father in heaven is absolutely
directing the most minute circumstances of our
short sojourn in this wilderness world! That nothing,
however trivial, takes place, whether it relates to the
body or the soul, but is under His control—
in fact, is ordered by Himself!

MARY WINSLOW

*N*ot long ago we were invited to a dinner meeting at an up-
scale restaurant in downtown Grand Rapids, Michigan.

When we arrived, we gave the maître d' the name of our party.
We were promptly escorted to a private room, where our server
greeted us warmly. Once we were seated, he handed each of us a
leather-bound menu with the name of the restaurant embossed
on the cover. Classy.

Then, opening the menus, we were surprised to encounter
the latest in touchscreen technology. Very cool.

We placed our orders, then settled into comfortable, uninterrupted conversation. In just the right amount of time, our server returned first with our appetizers and a little later with our salads. But when he returned the next time, he was accompanied by three additional waiters, who carried our entrées. This was the first time we had seen these other three, but they seemed to know exactly who had ordered what. This was especially impressive because the plates they were holding were covered with shiny chrome domes.

Placing our dinners in front of us, the four servers looked to each other for a signal. Then, at precisely the same moment, the silver covers were lifted . . . followed by a chorus of oohs and aahs. The entrées looking up at us after the big reveal were exactly what we had ordered.

Nicely done.

The problem is, when it comes to real life, what's on our plates under those chrome domes is often something we *didn't* order and might not even want. And because the selection on others' plates is clearly visible, we may be tempted to compare ours to theirs.

"That's not fair," we may protest. "This isn't what I wanted. Why didn't I get that dinner rather than this one?"

To make things worse, we may not have had a chance to "order" at all.

What we'd prefer would be to choose what looks good to us, our best-life-now hopes and dreams, and then to have the server return, lift the silver dome, and—voilà!—exactly what we wanted. And occasionally that may be the case. But sometimes it's not. Often it's not. God's divinely apportioned sovereignty is usually a surprise to us mortals.

So why would we trust a God who doesn't give us what we want?

In fact, why would a good, loving God serve up unappetizing portions to us?

You can keep your cancer. I'll take a pony.

❧

This book is about trusting God to write your story. But as we've said, this is really about God's Story. His ways. His watchful care over His creation. His Providence.

Providence—it's not a word you hear a lot in everyday conversation. In fact, a search of Google books shows that the use of the word in print has steadily declined since 1800. But it's an incredibly important word and concept.

Noah Webster's 1828 dictionary gives us insight into this bedrock truth that we need to learn to love and lean hard into:

> Foresight, timely care; particularly, active foresight . . . accompanied with the procurement of what is necessary for future use. . . . In theology, the care and superintendence which God exercises over his creatures.[1]

Tucked inside this three-syllable word is the shorter word *provide*, which combines the Latin *videre*, meaning "to see" (think "video") with the prefix *pro*, meaning "before." *Pro-video*, "to see before"—that's at the heart of God's Providence.

God goes before us. He sees and knows everything before it even happens. And He makes provision for whatever we will need at that time.

Stop and think about that for a moment. Imagine the peace, comfort, and hope that would be ours if we really believed that He knows and sees everything that lies before us, *before* it happens—and that He has already provided whatever we will need when we get there! What freedom from fear, anxiety, and dread that should give us.

This is why I (Nancy) often say, "I love living under Providence!" What an amazing gift this is to us.

⌒

If we were able to sit down with Jesus and chat about Providence, He might explain it with a simple word picture, much as He did on a Galilean hillside a long time ago:

> Look at the birds of the air: they neither sow nor reap nor gather into barns, and yet your heavenly Father feeds them. Are you not of more value than they? . . . Consider the lilies of the field, how they grow: they neither toil nor spin, yet I tell you, even Solomon in all his glory was not arrayed like one of these. (Matt. 6:26–29)

Birds. Wildflowers. Human beings. In His Providence, God sustains, attires, and cares for all of His creation.

⌒

Our home in southwest Michigan gives us a front-row seat to an amazing array of wildlife. Having lived here for almost four years at the publication of this book, I (Robert) have become a bird man. There are thousands of birds in our neighborhood, ranging from tiny yellow goldfinches to massive hawks, herons, and bald eagles. I revel in the sight of these amazing creatures just outside my window. And early in the morning, even in the dead of winter, you'll find me trudging through deep snow to refill the bird feeders, just to be sure our little feathered friends have breakfast.

But what if I didn't do this? Would the birds go hungry? And who feeds the birds I can't feed? Who looks out for them when I'm out of town?

The fact is, none of these winged creatures needs me in order to survive.

That's right. Our good, wise, sovereign God cares for and meets the needs of the smallest of His creatures. Every single day. That doesn't mean they never have problems or that they never get hurt. But Jesus assured us that even common, ordinary sparrows cannot fall to the ground and die apart from the "Father's consent" (Matt. 10:29 CSB). Even the birds live under Providence.

And then there are the flowers.

The first spring after our wedding, I received a call from Nancy.

"We need to hurry, honey," she said.

"What's up?" I queried.

"The trilliums are blooming," she explained. "And they'll only last for a few more days."

Not having any idea who or what trilliums were, I did my best to be a fully engaged husband and act like this was important. So I went along.

I could not have been prepared for the sight of hundreds of thousands of delicate little white flowers carpeting the floor of the wooded acreage just a few miles from our house. Taking Nancy's hand as we walked a narrow, winding path through the loveliness, I drank in the beauty and worshiped the Creator who designed this visual feast—for His own enjoyment and ours.

When Jesus wanted to help people understand and trust God's Providence, He reminded them that God does a more than adequate job of feeding birds and clothing flowers. So what does that mean for you? It means you have a God who cares deeply about you and who will meet your needs. He doesn't just watch the birds eat or take photos of white blossoms. He is personally involved with the feeding and clothing. And what He does for these, He will do for you.

But that's not all there is to God's Providence. The word also speaks to His wise, sovereign rule over every detail of His creation.

Now, this is admittedly a subject that can stir up animated arguments. But there are basically two options.

Either . . .

1. God sovereignly causes and/or permits everything to happen that happens in our lives and in this world.

Or . . .

2. God stands by and watches passively and powerlessly, unwilling or unable to do anything about what happens.

> Where would we be without the certain knowledge that "He's got the whole world in His hands" and that every detail of our lives and days is ordered by our all-wise, all-knowing, loving God?

So here at the outset, we're going to be clear that *we choose door number one.*

Where would we be without the certain knowledge that "He's got the whole world in His hands" and that every detail of our lives and days is ordered by our all-wise, all-knowing, loving God? Far from being a crushing burden to be borne or diminishing our value, the Providence of God is a great and precious gift. To be helpless victims of chance, tossed about on the storms of life—that would be forever disconcerting and tragic. Thank God it is not the case.

As Pastor Charlie Dates tweeted recently after experiencing a turbulent flight:

> I'm amazed at how, on a bumpy flight, the pilot's voice
> is calm and assured when addressing the passengers.
> What unnerves us doesn't seem to bother them. It's good
> to have a life captain who's assured of your safe arrival when
> life is bumpy.[2]

The Old Testament book of Exodus includes many providential moments. One of the most dramatic was when the Israelites were finally released from their Egyptian captors. They were escaping eastward, but there was a problem. They came to a massive body of water, with no way over or around it—and no boats or life jackets. What's more, a ferocious army was bearing down on them, brandishing swords and plenty of hostility.

In the next few hours, God's Providence would be on display in a way that makes bird feeding and flower dressing look like child's play. But His people didn't trust that it would happen. In spite of God's relentless faithfulness up to that point, in spite of watching Yahweh perform one spectacular miracle after another on their behalf, they feared for their lives and fell back into their trademark response: complaining. "So dying in Egypt wasn't good enough for you?" they griped to Moses as they stood there on the banks of the Red Sea. "You just want us to die here in the wilderness?" (see Exod. 14:11–12).

Undaunted, Moses had another plan. He trusted God. Proving that he was the right man for the job, he announced to the restless, fearful mob:

> Fear not, stand firm, and see the salvation of the LORD....
> The LORD will fight for you, and you have only to be silent.
> (Exod. 14:13–14)

And show up He did. Not only did He provide a path through the water and drown the pursuing army, He went on to lead the ragtag group of Israelites through the wilderness, providing food, water, protection, and more until they finally reached the land He had promised them.

Shades of watching God feed our birds or staring in awe at the little white wildflowers spread out in the woods.

Our heavenly Father looks at our circumstances, our concerns, and our anxious fears, and says, "Take heart, My child. I've got this."

A close friend of ours has been walking through some horrifically messy and painful circumstances—mostly the fallout of the sins of others. In a recent text exchange, I (Nancy) wrote to her:

> When things seem to be falling apart, it's natural to freak out, hyperventilate, give in to fear, anger, or despair, or try to wrestle the problems down and get them out of your life. But this moment is part of a bigger Story He is writing in and through you. Remember the Red Sea. Stand still. See the salvation of the Lord.

Our heavenly Father looks at our circumstances, our concerns, and our anxious fears, and says, "Take heart, My child. I've got this."

God's Providence is often better seen in retrospect.

There's something about the clarity of looking into a rearview mirror. Looking back often gives us a more accurate picture of where we've been and what it means. That's not to say that every look back will show us all there is to see—at least not in this life. We have to have eyes to see, and that may take time and prayer. But if we continue to ponder where we've been and look with the eyes of faith, the view in the rearview mirror will often snap into focus and we'll get a clearer vision of how God has been working in our lives.

The view out the front windshield is a different story. We may think we know where we're headed, only to discover again and again that we had no earthly idea. What actually takes place may not at all be what we had envisioned or anticipated.

What we see looking ahead is our story—our circumstances seen from our finite, limited perspective.

What appears when we look back is God's Story—what He sees and knows and has in mind, how He is always at work for our good and His glory.

God is writing a Story—the Story of redemption. It is grander and greater than anything we can imagine. Here are some important things we need to remind ourselves often about His Story and how it relates to the story He is writing in and through each of our lives:

1. *Our individual stories are part of a much bigger Story.* At times, we will experience heartache, loss, disappointment, and unfulfilled longings. But He is weaving all of that into a Story that will have us lost in wonder and worship when we get to the end.

2. *Ultimately, this Story is not about us, but about Him.* We are bit players in His Story. We are not the stars. He is!

3. *Perspective makes all the difference.* God sees the beginning and the end and everything in between; we only see this present moment. In storytelling language, His is an

omniscient point of view, whereas ours is limited to what we can perceive from our earthly vantage point. He has a wide-angle lens and sees the whole mural He is painting in all of history. We see only the little speck of time and space we occupy at this moment.

4. *God works in unexpected, unexplainable ways to accomplish His purposes.* We should not expect Him to write our story the way we would write it.

5. *God sovereignly and purposefully ordains and orchestrates the circumstances of our lives.* There is no such thing as happenstance or accident. Nothing catches Him off guard. There is no plot twist in your story or ours of which He is unaware or that He can't overcome.

6. *What we see now is not the whole story.* If we could see what God sees and know what He knows, our hearts would be at peace.

7. *We can trust Him to write the story of those we love.* That doesn't mean we shouldn't help or support them. But we don't want to rescue them from circumstances that may be a chapter of the story He is writing in their lives.

8. *The challenges we face may be a part of God writing someone else's story.* God wants to use our story to be a means of His grace and intervention in the lives of others—even those who may have "wrecked" our story.

9. *Those who trust in Him will never be disappointed.*[3] Not every chapter in this life has a "happy" ending. But every true child of God will live "happily ever after." We can be sure of that.

10. *You can trust God to write your story* . . . and you can be sure that in the end, He will *right* your story!

The biblical account of Job is a stunning story of God's control over the events of our world and the happenings in our lives.

The book that bears his name opens with a ringing endorsement of Job's character: "blameless and upright, one who feared God and turned away from evil" (Job 1:1). Yet, this God-loving, sin-hating man—a devoted family man and generous benefactor—was not insulated from agonizing suffering and loss.

To the contrary, in a test of divine sovereignty that really had nothing directly to do with Job, God gave Satan permission to afflict this godly man with unimaginable loss and pain. One unanticipated disaster after another hit Job hard from every direction and caused the bottom to fall out. His great wealth—gone in a day. His ten (!) children—all dead in a moment. His body—covered with excruciating sores. His wife (also suffering deep grief)—confused and disoriented. His friends—misguided and unhelpful at best.

> What we see now is not the whole story. If we could see what God sees and know what He knows, our hearts would be at peace.

At the outset, Job held fast to his confidence that God is worthy to be blessed, not just when He is the dispenser of blessings, but also when those good gifts are removed and replaced with adversity. But as time wore on, that confidence sometimes wavered. Through thirty-five chapters of endless dialogue and debating about the problem of pain, Job's inspiring bursts of faith were interspersed with anguished outbursts of questioning and despair. And all the while God was silent. As hard as Job and his well-meaning friends tried to figure all this out, they just didn't know what they didn't know.

Finally, the sovereign God stepped forward and addressed His suffering servant: "You've pummeled me with questions," the Lord said in effect. "Now, I have a few questions for you!"

> I will ask you, and you instruct Me! (Job 38:3 NASB)

For starters . . .

> Where were you when I laid the foundation of the earth?
> Tell Me, if you have understanding. (v. 4 NASB)

Then, for the next four chapters, God held court. In one incontestable point after another, He reminded Job of His track record as the Lord of all creation. He unveiled His greatness, His power, and His providential oversight and care of the universe. Job interrupted only once—to acknowledge that he was way out of his league when it came to understanding or challenging God:

> Behold, I am insignificant; what can I reply to You?
> I lay my hand on my mouth. (40:4 NASB)

Finally, when he had heard God out, Job responded in resignation, confession, and humble, awe-filled wonder:

> I know that You can do all things,
> And that no purpose of Yours can be thwarted. . . .
> I have declared that which I did not understand,
> Things too wonderful for me, which I did not know. . . .
> I had heard of You by the hearing of the ear;
> But now my eye sees You. . . .
> Therefore I retract,
> And I repent. (42:2–6 NASB)

In other words, "You win. You are good. You are faithful. I trust You to write my story."

Chances are, your story is not as dramatic as Job's, yet your problems and your pain are no less real. You may not be able to see His purposes or plan at this point. But by His grace, you can rest in His Providence, confident that . . .

He is good.

He is faithful.

And you can trust Him to write your story.

CHAPTER 2

Chosen

Esther's Story

Just like a diamond glistens most brightly
when placed on the backdrop of darkness,
God's glory displays brightly
as He brings about divine reversals.

TONY EVANS

It may surprise you to discover that one of the books of the Bible that most prominently showcases the Providence of God does not include His name. The Old Testament book of Esther is one of only two books that makes no specific reference to God. (The other one is the Song of Songs.) But the entire story of Esther bears the unmistakable imprint of His presence and His activity. It's just a small part of God's far greater Story that encompasses all of time, space, and eternity. But it also mirrors and gives us a glimpse of that larger Story.

This is an account of the way God intervened supernaturally to deliver His chosen people from annihilation through the courageous appeal of a Jewish orphan-girl-turned-queen. A girl named Esther.

The opening verse of the book tells us that these events took place "in the days of Ahasuerus" (Est. 1:1). Also known as Xerxes, this Persian king reigned over a world empire with borders reaching "from India to Ethiopia" (1:1).

Possessing raw, unchecked power, this monarch asserted absolute authority through irrevocable royal decrees. He flaunted his wealth with intimidating displays of opulence and high living. In fact, as the story opens, Ahasuerus was in the middle of a huge party, a six-month bender he threw for himself. What a guy. Can you imagine?

In the midst of these festivities, the king decided to show off Vashti, his trophy wife, to his drunken friends. Unwilling to be used in this way, she refused to come. And the imperial thug, angered by her rejection, summarily deposed his queen.

He was the king. He had the power. And though she had a royal position many might have envied, at the end of the day, this queen was no more than a pawn to be placed or replaced as he wished. Like most women of her era (and still today in some parts of the world), she was powerless to control her own destiny. She was subject to the conventions of her culture and to the whims of a dictatorial, heavy-drinking, easily angered, power-crazed husband and king.

This is the setting into which Esther would be placed. Humanly speaking, she would have no more control over her own future than Vashti had over hers.

But things are not always as they seem here on earth. *Heaven rules.* An unseen hand controls those who think they exercise ultimate control. Kings and kingdoms, laws and decrees—these are all subject to the One who sits on the throne and reigns over all. No human is powerful enough to thwart God's plan.

With the queen's throne now an empty chair, Ahasuerus decided to replace her by hosting a beauty pageant of sorts. But instead of being required to walk the runway and answer questions about world peace on live TV, one at a time these contestants would be forced to spend the night with him, and the one who "[pleased] the king" would become his queen (2:4).

How awful was this system of using and treating women like chattel for the purposes and pleasures of a powerful ruler? Ahasuerus issued orders for "all the beautiful young virgins" (v. 3) to be gathered, put under the supervision of the "keeper of the women," and taken through required beauty regimens to get them ready for their "auditions." Though some of them may have considered this a coveted honor, the fact is they had no real choice. Stripped of independence, they were to be used for someone else's pleasure and then discarded if they didn't measure up to his scrutiny. This king was a monster.

Where was God in all of this? And where is He today when depraved men objectify women and use them for their lustful purposes?

> Things are not always as they seem here on earth. *Heaven rules.* An unseen hand controls those who think they exercise ultimate control.

The story of Esther points us toward the answer. For while Ahasuerus was going about his brutal business—intent on world domination, exercising iron-fisted control over his subjects, and having his way with as many women as he wished, God was working to bring about judgment on the wicked as well as salvation for His people.

Enter Esther. Her young life had already been marked by the twin tragedies of being orphaned and living in exile from the Jewish homeland. We are also told that she was a virgin and that she was very beautiful—which put her in the crosshairs of the king's evil scheme. Esther was "taken" into the palace (2:8) and sequestered in the king's harem to be primped and prepared for a night with the king.

Though she may have felt abandoned and alone, separated from all that was familiar, Esther was being watched by someone who deeply cared for her. Each day her only living relative, her cousin and guardian Mordecai, paced back and forth in front of the harem's courtyard. He had to know how Esther was doing and "what was happening to her" (2:11).

Mordecai's watchful care over his adopted cousin is a picture of the God who is the Keeper of those who belong to Him. He faithfully watches over us, never sleeping (see Ps. 121:3–4). When we are "imprisoned" in circumstances out of our control, even if the result is of our own doing, we are never alone; we are not invisible. We may feel we are at a dead end, trapped, no way out, no future or hope. But our "heavenly Mordecai" is there. Though often unseen by us, His care is certain. Every day He "walks by" our place. He watches what is happening to us and "learns" how we are doing. Unlike Mordecai, however, He isn't powerless to help. Instead, He is working behind the scenes, making arrangements, putting everything in place. And in time, He will be the means of upending our enemy's objectives and fulfilling God's holy purpose for our lives.

Unlike the caring Mordecai, King Ahasuerus was an unworthy man who used women to satisfy his lust. He "tried" women for one night, and if they did not please him, they would spend the rest of their lives in a second harem as one of the king's concubines, never again to go to the king (or any other man).

This is sheer evil, of course, but it's not unheard of, even today, for women not to be recognized as being created in the image of God (*imago dei*). The details may change, but the tragic brokenness continues. For now.

One day, however, every vile practice in our broken, fallen world will be done away with and all things will be made new. And in the meantime, God is always mindful of His own, always redeeming, always acting to bring about His kingdom purposes—in His way and His time.

Esther was not rescued out of the king's perverse system. But she was cared for by One higher than the king, even while living as

> One day every vile practice in our broken, fallen world will be done away with and all things will be made new.

the king's prisoner. By God's Providence, she "gained favor" in the harem and then before Ahasuerus. He "loved Esther more than all the women" and made her queen, putting her in a unique position to help her people.

Her Father knew what He was doing. He was writing Esther's story . . . and the story of an entire generation of His chosen ones, oblivious as they were to His presence and care.

⟋‿⟍

Not long after Esther was made queen, divine Providence spun another plot thread in her story. Mordecai overheard an assassination plot and told Esther, who reported it to the king. The culprits were caught, and the king's life was saved (2:21–23). But

Mordecai's good deed went unrecognized (for the time being) because a conniving, self-promoting official named Haman the Agagite gained the king's favor (3:1). And so it often is in real life. Faithful service goes unrewarded, while evil people with nefarious schemes are honored and exalted.

From earth's vantage point, Mordecai was a nobody against the backdrop of a massive, totalitarian regime. But in the Story God was writing, he played a significant role. Through his faithfulness and integrity an insidious plot would be averted and the people of God—from whom the Savior of the world would one day come—would be spared.

But we're getting ahead of our story.

The clash between good and evil continued to intensify. Haman's power and influence increased, and everyone in the kingdom was ordered to pay him homage. But Mordecai refused to bow down to Haman. The text in the book of Esther doesn't say exactly why, but a clue may be found in the fact that Haman was identified as an Agagite. This could mean that he was a descendent or relative of Agag, a sworn enemy of God and His people back in the days of Saul. Mordecai may have refused to bow down because he was unwilling to compromise his identity as a Jew.[1]

Whatever the reason, Mordecai's refusal to bow infuriated Haman, who schemed to destroy not only Mordecai but all the Jewish people. He convinced King Ahasuerus to issue an irreversible edict to "destroy, to kill, and to annihilate all Jews, young and old, women and children" (3:13). But neither the king nor Haman had any idea that the beautiful queen was among those destined for slaughter.

Haman and his henchmen had already "cast Pur"—like flipping a coin or rolling a dice—to determine the date of the genocide, so the law was issued with that deadline. Then the king and Haman "sat down to drink," celebrating their awful scheme while "the city . . . was thrown into confusion" (v. 15).

When the Jews throughout the kingdom learned of the king's decree, there was "great mourning . . . with fasting and weeping and lamenting, and many of them lay in sackcloth and ashes" (4:3). This is significant to note, because these events took place during a spiritual low in the history of God's people. He sometimes uses even the evil intentions of His adversaries to bring His people to a place of humility and desperation, recognizing their dependence on Him for deliverance. And certainly no scenario could be more dire, more hopeless, than what the Jewish people faced after Ahasuerus made his decree!

But *heaven rules.* Then and now, no matter how desperate the circumstances seem, God is writing His Story. Kings and evil men may rage and initiate their schemes, but they can do nothing that He does not permit for His own greater purposes. And when God decides to do so, He can and will undo all the damage His enemies seek to do to His people.

Mordecai appealed to Esther to use her royal standing to plead for the life of her people. Sadly, she was not in a position to do so, as the king had not summoned her for a month. To go before him without such a summons would place her at great personal risk, because anyone who entered the king's inner court without being summoned could be put to death. But she agreed to try—which created a perfect opportunity for divine intervention.

It came with precise, split-second timing. God orchestrated a sequence of events, some of them seemingly random and insignificant:

- The king couldn't sleep.
- To pass the time, he ordered a book to be brought in from the royal archives and read to him.

- The book contained a record of Mordecai stopping an assassination plot against the king.

- At that very moment Haman walked in, intending to get the king's approval to hang his nemesis, Mordecai, on a towering gallows he had ordered to be built for that purpose. . . .

You can't make this stuff up!

Now the tables began to be turned—for both Haman and Mordecai. Haman, who had assumed the king would want to honor him above all men, ended up forced to publicly honor Mordecai, whom he loathed and whose destruction he had been in the process of engineering. His exhilaration over his favored status with the king spiraled to dejection, and his wife made things worse by (accurately) predicting that her husband would not overcome Mordecai, but instead would "surely fall" before him (6:13).

The way was now prepared for Esther to enter the king's presence, to plead for her own life and the lives of her people, and to expose the evil man who had orchestrated the whole wicked plan. Here was a vulnerable woman courageously standing in the flow of God's sovereign plan . . . "for such a time as this" (4:14).

Haman quickly went from being intoxicated with power and wine to being "terrified." In a dramatic reversal, the one who had schemed and made plans to destroy the lives of those who resisted him was himself destroyed. In fact, "they hanged Haman on the gallows that he had prepared for Mordecai" (7:10).

God vindicates His own. The words of the psalmist are true:

> A little while, and the wicked person will be no more. . . .
> But the humble will inherit the land
> and will enjoy abundant prosperity.
>
> The wicked person schemes against the righteous
> and gnashes his teeth at him.
> The Lord laughs at him
> because he sees that his day is coming. . . .
>
> The wicked will perish . . .
> they will fade away like smoke. (Ps. 37:10–13, 20 csb)

Mordecai, once abased, was now lifted up by the king. He was given authority to issue a counteredict giving the Jews authority to arm and defend themselves. On the very day the Jewish genocide was to take place, Mordecai was greatly honored, promoted to second-ranking official in the land, while the one who had sought to destroy him was humiliated, demoted, and executed. One of Mordecai's first official acts was to institute an annual festival to commemorate "the days on which the Jews got relief from their enemies, and as the month that had been turned for them from sorrow into gladness and from mourning into a holiday" (9:22).[2]

Haman had plotted "to crush and to destroy" the Jews (v. 24). He had even cast lots ("pur") to determine the day it would all go down. But events on this earth are never determined by chance. As the nineteenth-century hymn writer Maltbie Babcock put it:

> This is my Father's world.
> O let me ne'er forget
> That though the wrong seems oft so strong,
> God is the ruler yet.[3]

Esther's story reveals it. Our stories can as well.
Heaven rules.

Graced

Our Story

A providence is shaping our ends;
a plan is developing in our lives;
a supremely wise and loving Being
is making all things work together for good.

F. B. MEYER

Our story is really a tale of two families, beginning with two couples: Samuel and Grace Wolgemuth and Arthur and Nancy DeMoss.

Both couples called Pennsylvania home for a time.

Both loved Christ, His Word, and His people.

Both shared a passion for the whole world to know "the old, old story of Jesus and His love."[1]

And both couples left a remarkable legacy of faith and faithfulness for their families and for the generations that would follow them.

In 1948, Sam and Grace gave birth to their fourth child,

Robert David. Twins would follow seven years later, completing this family of eight.

Ten years after Robert made his entrance into the world—exactly nine months and four days after their wedding—Art and Nancy DeMoss welcomed a daughter, who they named after her mother. Within the first five years of their marriage, God would bless them with six children, with a seventh born several years later.

Both couples wholly surrendered their lives and plans to Christ, resolved to follow Him wherever He led. And both talked openly and often with their children about the Scripture, Christ, and the gospel. Though these families didn't know each other at the time, in His inscrutable wisdom and plan, the Lord would one day intertwine their stories.

Looking now in the rearview mirror, we can see the unmistakable Providence of God—how He used our families and our experiences to shape our young hearts, steer the course of our lives, and prepare us for a lifetime of service . . . and an eternity of joy.

We marvel as we reflect on His intimate involvement in every chapter, every scene, every detail of our story.

ROBERT'S STORY *(as told by Nancy)*

Back in the 1940s, Robert's dad sold farm equipment for the Frick Company, headquartered in the small town of Waynesboro, Pennsylvania. In his midthirties, with little formal theological training, Samuel agreed to become the pastor of a dwindling Brethren in Christ congregation. This meant preaching on weekends and Wednesday nights and being on call, as any small-town minister understands, whenever a parishioner had a need.

At his side, always, was Robert's tall, elegant mother, Grace Dourte Wolgemuth, a licensed practical nurse. In fact, Samuel always introduced his wife as "Grace, by my side." Samuel leaned heavily on his wife's gentle way with people, and those who knew her wondered at her gifts of hospitality and homemaking.

In later years, "Lady Grace" would be loved around the globe as she accompanied Samuel on many of his travels as president of Youth for Christ, International. When Robert spoke at his mother's funeral in 2010, he began, "Her parents named her Grace. How did they know?"

Though not particularly outgoing, young Robert was a likable kid. He loved climbing trees on their property in Waynesboro, as well as (depending on the time of year) riding his bike or sledding on Frick Avenue, which sloped downhill from their home.

Each Sunday, Robert and his siblings would sit dutifully in church, lined up on a wooden pew near the front of the sanctuary, while their father preached. Sam Wolgemuth was not a dynamic communicator, but his sincere passion for the gospel came through clearly. The way he began each sermon is indelibly etched in Robert's memory.

> We marvel as we reflect on His intimate involvement in every chapter, every scene, every detail of our story.

Walking across the low platform at the front of the sanctuary, Samuel would place his large black Bible and notes on the pulpit, then step to the side and take a knee. Sometimes he would invite the congregation to join him by kneeling at their pews. Then he would call on the Lord to give him wisdom as he opened the Word.

Prayer was not just a public performance for this preacher

dad. Robert recalls many mornings of lying in bed in his first-floor bedroom and hearing the muffled tones of his father praying downstairs in the basement family room. Though unable to make out the exact words, this son knew that nothing mattered more to his dad than seeking and receiving the favor of God.

His dad's model of humility and prayer had a profound impact on Robert's life.

When Robert was just four years old, his family went to see *Mr. Texas*, a semiautobiographical film starring Christian country singer/songwriter/actor Redd Harper. As Robert watched it, the Spirit of God moved in his young heart. Before they left that evening, he knelt next to his mother, both of them in tears, and committed his life to Christ—the beginning of a whole new life with eternal implications.

Months later, Sam and Grace and their (then) four children, ages four through eleven, boarded a ship bound for Japan. They were embarking on a new adventure, a two-year assignment with Youth for Christ. Robert remembers his parents' selling or giving away virtually everything they owned prior to leaving their home in Pennsylvania in order to say yes to God's call. This was another formative moment that would mark him with a lifelong conviction that Christ is worthy of our wholehearted devotion and that loving, following, and serving Him is our highest duty and joy.

When the family returned from their time overseas, they settled in Wheaton, Illinois, for Robert's dad to take on the role of Youth for Christ's Overseas Director.

Sam and Grace were eager for their children to develop a strong work ethic from an early age. From third through ninth grade (until he got a better-paying job at one dollar per hour), Robert had a paper route that got him up before daylight six mornings a week. Sitting on the cold garage floor, he would roll up a hundred copies of the *Chicago Tribune*, then carry them in a basket mounted on the front of his heavy-duty Schwinn bike, carefully aiming them at the front porches of his customers' homes.

After high school Robert attended Taylor University, a Christian liberal arts college in north-central Indiana, as had his parents before him (and as have thirty-two Wolgemuths to date). Hopelessly entrepreneurial, Robert helped pay his way through school by selling custom-made dress shirts, corsages, and diamonds imported from Asia from his dorm room.

A highlight of his college years was climbing back on a Schwinn—a sleeker model than the paper-route edition—the summer before his senior year and riding nearly four thousand miles, from San Francisco to New York City (no interstates!). He rode with thirty-nine other students, a group that called themselves "The Wandering Wheels." Some of those men continue to be among Robert's closest friends.

Robert's interest in science had led him to start out as a pre-med student. But during his third year, he sensed a call to ministry and changed his major, graduating in 1969 with a degree in biblical literature. Then, for the next nine years, he served with Youth for Christ, first as a high school club director, then on the staff of *Campus Life* magazine.

His work at the magazine was the beginning of a career in Christian publishing, which has included key management roles at two different publishers, starting a publishing company with his business partner, authoring more than twenty books, and in 1992 starting a literary agency that today represents more than two hundred Christian authors.

One of the greatest joys of Robert's life is teaching God's Word—something he did weekly in adult Sunday school classes for more than thirty years.

Over and over again, since the first time I heard Robert's name around the year 2000, ministry leaders, colleagues in the publishing industry, and many among his family and friends have told me how greatly they respect this man and how grateful they are for the imprint he has left on their lives.

Nancy's Story *(as told by Robert)*

Nancy Leigh (called by both names as a child to distinguish her from her mother, also named Nancy) always loved school. Actually, what she really loved was learning. While other kids were on the swing set or kicking a ball around, Nancy could usually be found sitting on the sidelines or in her room reading a book.

Her first conscious memory is of the afternoon of May 14, 1963, when, at age four she turned to Christ to save her. That day she gave all that she knew of herself to all that she knew of Him. And there was no turning back.

From those early years as a child of God, Nancy sensed the Lord's hand on her life and the call to serve Him, though she had no idea what that might look like down the road. In our living room sits a framed letter Nancy wrote to her parents when she was seven years old. (Though a champion speller even at that age, she misspelled "missionary" as "missonary" each of the seven times it appeared in the original letter!):

> Dear Mommy and Daddy,
> On Saturday I knew that God had touched my heart and wanted me to be a missionary for him, and it was just as if he had stood before me.
> Right then I started to think what and how a mission-

ary would speak to people. I could just tell everybody this wonderful news. I am so happy about it. And I just know that God has spoken to me and told me to be a missionary for him. And I think that being a missionary is the best job for me.

And I am so happy that God wants me to be a missionary for him.

I hope that God is going to help me be a missionary. It's just as God saying to me: Go, Nancy, go Nancy. You can do it. You can do it. Be a missionary for me. Go, Nancy, go Nancy.

Love,
Nancy Leigh

P.S. Go into all the world and preach the gospel. I'm going to do it for Jesus and Jesus only shall I do it for.

Nancy's heart for the world was expanded through a number of opportunities during her childhood to join her parents on ministry trips to other countries. Her businessman dad had a tireless heart for ministry and a great burden for people everywhere to hear the gospel. He longed for his family to share this zeal. So he and his wife would take their children with them on "ministry vacations," where they could participate in various evangelistic and ministry endeavors, see firsthand the lostness of people without Christ, and witness the power of God to save and transform lives. Those trips had a significant and lasting impact on the life of their firstborn daughter.

Nancy Leigh didn't wait until she was grown up to begin fulfilling her call to serve the Lord. At age eight she was asked to fill in for her third-grade Sunday school teacher and then to teach children in Vacation Bible School. She was hooked. This young woman who loved sitting under the preaching of the Word almost more than anything else discovered that she also loved studying the Word on her own and teaching it to others, a passion that is undiminished to this day.

On her sixteenth birthday, at the beginning of her freshman year at Philadelphia College of Bible, Nancy received a letter from her beloved dad. He reflected on some of his early memories of his oldest child:

> I can hardly believe that you're now in college! I can still remember your first birthday, just fifteen years ago, at the Bible Conference at Winona Lake, Indiana—certainly a good way for one to start out in life!
>
> I remember when you were very little, how you always wanted to go wherever there was a gospel meeting in progress—whether it was a deacons' meeting or a rescue mission or the old ladies' home!

Nancy's dad also affirmed his desire for God to use her life in whatever ways He would choose:

> I've become increasingly convinced that God has something very special and very wonderful for you—which I know will become a reality, because you want only to know and to do God's will for your life.
>
> And believe me, I'd infinitely rather see you in the Lord's will than to be rich or famous or anything else! After all, it's really true, that there's
>
> Only one life, 'twill soon be past,
> Only what's done for Christ will last.[2]

For her last two years of college, Nancy transferred to the University of Southern California, where she graduated in 1978 with a degree in piano performance. During high school and college, she had remained actively involved in her church, pouring herself into ministering to children and their parents. After graduation, she joined the staff of a large church in Virginia as the Primary

Children's Ministry director. Through these years the Lord was deepening her heart for people and for faithful gospel ministry.

⌒

On Friday, August 31, 1979, at her dad's request, Nancy flew home to Philadelphia to celebrate her upcoming twenty-first birthday with her family. Returning to the house from dinner that evening, Nancy recalls her dad saying to a friend who had joined them, "You know, we may never be all together like this again."

The next morning, September 1, Art and Nancy DeMoss drove their firstborn to the airport for her flight back to Virginia. Her dad was dressed in his tennis gear for a doubles match he had scheduled with three men he had discipled in their walk with Christ.

Two hours later, when Nancy's plane landed, a friend met her with the news that her mother was trying to reach her.

"Daddy is in heaven," her now-widowed mother said when they connected. He had dropped dead of a heart attack on the tennis court—absent from the body, present with the Lord (2 Cor. 5:8). Stunned by the news, she quickly boarded another plane to rejoin her family.

Today, reflecting on her father's life and legacy, Nancy says, "He was a living illustration of the principles he taught us." This included giving the first hour of his day—every day—to the Lord in Bible reading and prayer, a habit that left an enduring mark on his daughter's heart.

⌒

Over the following years, God graced this gifted, single woman with a vibrant, fruitful career in ministry. In 1980, she left local church ministry and began traveling across America with Life Action Ministries, an organization that seeks to ignite Christ-centered movements of revival among God's people. Then, beginning in 2000, the Lord opened new opportunities for Nancy to become an author and the founder of Revive Our Hearts, now a worldwide ministry for women under the Life Action umbrella. Nancy's teaching program, which airs each weekday via podcast and on the Internet as well as over a thousand radio outlets, was launched as the successor program to Elisabeth Elliot's *Gateway to Joy* radio program.

In early 2015, Nancy told her closest friends that she was in a "good place." She loved pouring herself wholeheartedly into serving Him and others. She was grateful for the story God had written for her life thus far. And she was not looking for a husband.

OUR STORY

We were both blessed with the example of parents whose marriages, though imperfect, were strong. This was a rich gift of God's grace to each of us.

Though Nancy was a great champion of marriage and much of her ministry involved serving married women, for many years she had felt a sense of calling to serve the Lord as a single woman. While many might have felt this to be a burden, she truly considered it a blessing.

> Only God fully knows why He does what He does. But we know that whatever He does is purposeful, good, and for our ultimate joy.

I (Robert), on the other hand, had no doubt as a young man that someday I would be married. And as I got to know a beautiful, outgoing, and talented woman named Bobbie Gardner, I knew pretty quickly that she would be the one. In March of 1970, the two of us were married in Arlington, Virginia. Our daughter Missy was born in September of 1971, and three years later Julie made her appearance.

Bobbie and I shared life together for nearly forty-five years. Of course, there were times of testing. But those were sweet years, blessed with much growth and grace. Then, in His Providence, the Lord called Bobbie to heaven after a courageous thirty-month-long battle with ovarian cancer.

Knowing the aggressive progression of the cancer and that her days on this earth were few, Bobbie had made clear to her family and friends that she was eager for me to remarry. And a few weeks before she died in 2014, in two separate conversations, she told two friends, "I'd like Robert to marry Nancy Leigh DeMoss."

But she never told me.

Nancy and I had known each other professionally for a number of years. I had represented her as an author's agent from 2003 to 2005. She and Bobbie knew each other and shared a mutual love for the Lord, for hymns, for ministering to women, and more. Nancy had even interviewed Bobbie and me, along with one of our daughters and our oldest grandchild, for her radio program, where we talked about singing hymns as a family.

Not long after Bobbie was diagnosed with cancer, Nancy was speaking at a conference in Florida, where we lived, and she took time to visit Bobbie at our home. So Bobbie had seen Nancy's heart, and she had sensed that Nancy would be a suitable mate for me when she was gone. What a gracious gift that proved to be.

Though I did not know this had been in Bobbie's thinking, as I maneuvered through those difficult months following Bobbie's death, I sometimes found my thoughts turning toward Nancy. Eventually she and I began a correspondence that grew into a deepening friendship and, eventually, a courtship.

We both had a lot to work through in those early days—my grief over losing Bobbie, Nancy's calling as a single woman, our separate careers and ministries, even the geographical distance between us. But after much prayer, conversation, and seeking counsel from a few trusted friends, we both sensed a green light to begin dating. And two months later, the two women Bobbie had spoken with reached out and told me what Bobbie had said—that this is exactly what she had hoped would happen after her death.

It was becoming clear that the Lord was writing a new chapter in my life as well as Nancy's.

This was a story I (Nancy) had never envisioned for myself. But the Lord began to "awaken love" in the heart of this fifty-seven-year-old woman. As I earnestly sought His direction, there was a growing sense and finally a settled assurance that He was redirecting my life and entrusting me with a different gift—the gift of marriage. This would be a new avenue to experience and share the Story of His pursuing, redeeming love.

On a picture-perfect Saturday morning in May, Robert showed up at my house holding a large bouquet of roses. After sharing some Scripture and praying, he knelt before the couch where I was sitting and officially proposed marriage. My response was a simple, "Yes . . . with all my heart."

Then on November 14, 2015, before a congregation of more than five hundred friends (and tens of thousands more who joined online), we exchanged vows and were married. Eighty-year-old Dr. Bill Hogan, whom I had known since childhood, who had been my pastor during my high school and part of my college years, and from whom I received a deep love for expository

Bible preaching, officiated at our wedding. The front of the (twenty-eight-page!) program read:

A Celebration of Marriage:
A Portrait of God's Redeeming, Covenant-Keeping Love

Shining a spotlight on that picture, telling that Story, is the point and the passion of our lives—both individually and together.

The first years of our marriage involved lots of adjustments for both of us—more like a seismic shift for Nancy, who had never been married before. We have experienced the joys and challenges of weaving two lives together, learning to love and serve each other well, trusting our loving Father who is writing a script neither of us could have imagined.

Nancy's ministry produced a short video on our courtship and marriage. They called it "Unexpected Grace: Nancy and Robert's Story."[3] And that's how we would both describe our whole story—through many surprising twists and turns, from our childhoods all the way up to this season we find ourselves in now.

We never cease to be amazed at the wonder of the grace God has lavished on us day after day,

> He has been faithful in each chapter thus far. And we know that He will be faithful in each one yet to come, that His grace with be sufficient for wherever He leads us. Above all, our desire is that our lives will showcase the beauty and the goodness of His Story.

year after year—rescuing, redeeming, forgiving, blessing, renewing, restoring, helping, healing, leading, encouraging, strengthening, sanctifying, transforming, and so much more.

We realize that, in many senses, our story is an unusual one. We have been the recipients of a godly heritage and countless other blessings we did not earn and for which we can take no credit. While our paths have not been pain free, we have been spared—thus far—many hardships that others have had to endure. We are not more spiritual or deserving than they.

But at the end of the day, it is pointless and foolish to compare stories. God is sovereign. His ways are unfathomable and inscrutable. Only He fully knows why He does what He does. But we know that whatever He does is purposeful, good, and for our ultimate joy. That is the heart of this book.

As we (Robert and Nancy) sit here today, we have no idea what our future may hold. Our story is still being written, and He has not given us an inside track on what the next chapters look like. But our trust is in the One who holds our future—the "author and finisher of our faith" (Heb. 12:2 NKJV). That gives us freedom and peace, even when we cannot see what lies ahead.

As we've listened to some of the painful stories dear friends have shared with us for this book, we can't help but wonder what rocky paths we may yet be called to travel. (We know it's impossible to become like Jesus apart from testing and trials.) We may yet face serious health issues, losing one or the other to death, and/or other crises known only to Him.

But we know He has been faithful in each chapter thus far. And we know that He will be faithful in each one yet to come, that His grace will be sufficient for wherever He leads us.

We don't want to tell Him how to write our story; we trust Him to write our story for us. Our goal is not to make a name, a ministry, or a reputation for ourselves, but to make much of Him and to finish the race He has marked out for us to run.

Above all, our desire is that our lives will showcase the beauty and the goodness of His Story.

CHAPTER 4

You Can Trust God When Your Marriage Is in Trouble

*We experience so little of the joy that sustains us in suffering
and the hope that anchors us amid shattered dreams
when we come to Him looking for the pathway out of hardships
instead of the pathway into His presence.*

LARRY CRABB

*E*very marriage starts out with hopes and dreams. But when those hopes are crushed and the dreams turn to dust through rejection, betrayal, or neglect, it can be painfully difficult to trust in God's providential love and care. If that's true for you—or someone you love—the following stories can serve as an encouragement and a reminder that God is faithful and loving, no matter what happens in your closest relationships.

"Carla and Michael" have been married for over forty years. When they started out, Carla was convinced that Michael, a man with plenty of financial means, was her ticket to happiness. But things didn't quite work out that way. In fact, Carla and Michael

have been separated three times. Two of those times were the result of his addictions and substance abuse.

During their second separation, in the mid-1980s, Carla and Michael both came to faith in Christ. But Michael's ongoing struggle with substance abuse continued to disrupt their marriage. And four months before their forty-first anniversary, they separated for a third time. Carla's heart was broken: "I'm nearly sixty-five," she said. "I don't know if I can go through this again!"

Ten years earlier, Carla had begged Michael to stop drinking. And for ten years he had lied to her, drinking behind her back, partying in secret, missing key life and family events, and frequently falling ill because of too much alcohol. For all practical purposes, Michael had checked out of his life and marriage. Carla couldn't trust anything he said or did. So she learned to do life on her own and make her own plans. There was no more "we" in the marriage.

In response to the dysfunction and hurt, Carla acknowledges, "I became a 'control girl.' It was a struggle to keep trusting God to work in our lives and marriage." But she clung to the truth expressed by author Jerry Bridges: "Because His love cannot fail, He will allow into our lives only the pain and heartache that is for our ultimate good."[1] And as she pressed into God's Word day after day, her heart was encouraged with His promises. She remembers:

> I typed a list of all these verses and carried it around with me, clutching it to my heart, memorizing the verses, and trusting God to do what His Word says. I began to trust Him for who He is, rather than relying on Him for a particular outcome, like my husband's sobriety or a restored marriage.

Carla asked the Lord to help her to desire Him above all else, even more than she longed for her husband, who was still in rehab as the Christmas season began.

They were apart for the holidays and for her sixty-fifth birthday.

She cried every day, waves of deep sorrow washing over her, some days feeling hopeless, still unsure about their future. She spent time reflecting on their forty years of marriage—the many struggles, hardships, dashed hopes and desires, as well as the many wonderful times. After Michael spent three months in rehab, she and Michael began counseling together with a godly professional. And she prayed constantly.

In the process, her heart continued to soften toward her husband, and she learned to live one day at a time, trusting God for every tomorrow. She wrote to me at one point:

> I placed my situation before the Lord, knowing that I am
> His child, and prayed: "O Lord, You are for marriage. This
> situation is beyond me. I give it to You for You to do what
> only You can do, so that You are glorified" (2 Kings 19:15–19).

Throughout the most difficult times, she experienced the nearness and goodness of the Lord:

> I am deeply humbled by God's intimate care for me, that He
> attends to my every need, that He promised to never leave or
> forsake me (Deut. 31:6). That He calls me by name and that
> I am holy and dearly loved in His sight (Col. 3:12). That I
> am secure in Him regardless of my circumstances. That God
> is my great reward (Gen. 15:1). That His love satisfies my
> deepest needs.

During what turned into a nearly yearlong separation, there were some painfully hard days, but there were also some really sweet ones—the kind of days she had stopped hoping for. During that journey, she shared with me,

> In this season the Lord has graciously drawn me closer to
> Him than ever before. I praise Him for the pain and for
> the areas needing repentance that He continues to reveal.

His mercies are new every morning (Lam. 3:23)! He is the restorer and the repairer (Ruth 4:15; Isa. 58:12). He alone is worthy to write my story.

"And I'm trying not to be a 'control girl'!" she added with a smiley emoji.

After a year of sobriety, Michael moved back home. Recently Carla texted me with an encouraging update:

Tomorrow is our forty-second anniversary—and it's a wow! We are only together by the grace of God. Brand new marriage. Better than ever. Honestly I didn't think it was possible to have this kind of relationship with Michael. I continue to be amazed by God and my brand-new husband. The Lord has led me into a rest and peace I've not experienced before. Ephesians 3:20!!!!

Michael and Carla's story is still being written—as is our story and as is yours. There will be more tests and challenges ahead, as their lives and marriage are being molded to be more like Jesus. But they have experienced the power of His covenant-keeping love to make all things new. They have witnessed His power to turn a mess into a miracle. And God is giving them a message of grace to share with others.

> This couple has witnessed His power to turn a mess into a miracle. And God is giving them a message of grace to share with others.

"Raquel" has not (yet) seen a miracle in the mess of her marriage. But she, like Carla, has been given a message of grace to

share. She and *"Fernando"* met in college in Southern California. Both from solid Christian homes, they became friends through a campus ministry. They married the week after graduation.

Raquel dreamed of growing old with Fernando, having children together, and being in fruitful ministry together. Soon after they were married, however, Raquel discovered a deep level of anger in Fernando that she had not seen before. A "very unhappy person," Fernando would ice Raquel, perpetually refusing to talk with her or their two girls, even at meals, all while living under the same roof. He also became obsessively controlling about every detail of their lives, erupting in fits of rage for any little reason or no reason at all. And when he wasn't working, he spent practically every waking moment in his recliner, eyes glued to the TV, compulsively switching channels, so as not to miss a single sporting event.

Afraid of rousing his anger, Raquel tended to push issues under the rug rather than confronting them. She didn't want to jeopardize the marriage she had dreamed of having, the beautiful family she desperately wanted.

This went on for years, with Raquel "stuffing" her anxiety and shielding others from the truth. But she finally realized she had to get honest about the fact that her marriage was broken. She shared her situation with a wise counselor—an incredibly emotional step but also a tremendously freeing one.

With the counselor's encouragement, she finally got the courage to open her heart to her husband, lovingly sharing her concerns. But as she had feared, he grew furious and walked out, leaving her weeping on the floor.

This whole cycle would be repeated again and again over their twenty-eight years of marriage. "You don't know you've created an idol out of your husband until something like this happens," she told us.

Ultimately, after many rounds of counseling and endless one-sided effort, Raquel and Fernando's marriage ended in a divorce Raquel didn't want and had fought hard to avoid. But her broken marriage is not her whole story, and it is not the end of her story.

Today Raquel releases Fernando daily to the Lord, determined not to let her loss steal her joy and well-being. She prays for him, for his healing, and even, if the Lord were to bring it about, for restoration of their marriage. And she continues to serve the Lord and others, including her daughters and their families. Regular rhythms of walking, worship, prayer, praise, soaking in Scripture, rest, community with godly friends, staying connected to the church, and pouring into others' lives help her to keep from sinking into self-pity, anger, or despair while she waits to see how God will finish her story.

> Raquel knows that the hardships of this life are temporary, that the plans God has for her are good, and that all she has been through is preparing and fitting her for eternity with Him.

Over the years, her girls have witnessed Raquel's brokenness and tears, and they have had their own heartaches with their dad. But though Raquel supports them, she has steadfastly refused to disparage Fernando to them. Instead, she has let them hear her prayers for him. Thankfully, they are walking with the Lord today, married to godly men and raising their children to follow Christ.

"I can't credit myself for where my kids are today," Raquel told us. "I haven't led them by being strong but by all of us being weak, desperately needing a strong God."

Above all, Raquel focuses on Jesus. She has known deep hurt and rejection, but she is a woman of great hope, all of it centered on Him. She knows He will never forsake her. He gives her grace to put one foot in front of the other each day and to face the future in dependence on Him and with—yes—joy. She knows that the hardships of this life are temporary, that the plans God has for her are good, and that all she has been through is preparing and fitting her for eternity with Him.

Stories like the ones you've just read remind us of the heavy toll of sin and selfishness on relationships—whether our own or others'. Sometimes it seems that the shards of broken marriages are washing up all around us. But then we encounter someone like **Lorna Wilkinson,**[2] whose story reminds us that the grace and power of God really can restore broken lives and homes.

I (Nancy) met Lorna at a Houston, Texas, church where I was speaking. At the close of a gathering she stood and asked if she could share a brief testimony. For the next several minutes, we all sat spellbound, listening to her amazing story of grace and redemption.

Lorna and her husband, Pascal, were married for twenty-one years, and for many of those years, Pascal had been a good husband and father. But eventually, as in Carla's story, Pascal's alcohol abuse ravaged their home. For nine years Lorna lived with broken promises, lying, and the financial chaos caused by Pascal's obsessive drinking and chronic irresponsibility.

"I couldn't trust my husband anymore," Lorna recalled. "He would drop me off at work and then forget to pick me up. Sometimes I would be left there for hours, finally having to rent a hotel room close by. It was a very difficult situation. I endured to the point that I finally said, 'I can't take this anymore. I have to get out.'"

Lorna filed for divorce and asked her husband to leave. It was all she knew to do. Needing her own transportation, she purchased a used vehicle from a friend. The night she picked up the vehicle, the radio was tuned to a Christian station. She never listened to Christian radio, so she reached over to change the station. But as she did, "a conviction" came over her, and she could not touch the dial. So she listened . . . all the way home.

The radio was still on the next morning as Lorna drove to work, and this time *Revive Our Hearts* was playing. In God's Providence, my message that day was on forgiveness. I spoke of the fact that true love doesn't keep score (see 1 Cor. 13:5). As Lorna listened, she remembers, she "was completely broken."

After the program ended, the words she had heard continued to go around and around in her mind. She couldn't stop thinking about them. A couple of days later, while driving home from work, Lorna gave her life to Jesus.

Having received Christ's forgiveness, she knew she needed to forgive her husband. But it wasn't easy to release all the pain he had caused her and her children.

> I despised Pascal. I didn't want him to touch me. I wanted no part of that relationship. So I prayed, "God, you know my heart. And you know my feelings toward my husband. I do not like him. I do not love him. But I know that You are love. And I'm asking you to let Your love flow through me."

A few days later, she received a call from Pascal telling her he was very sick. Still frustrated and angry, she said, "Why are you calling me? Why don't you call 911?"

He must have done so, because the next thing she heard he was in the hospital. He had had a heart attack. The family gathered in the waiting room, unsure whether he would survive.

At that point God began to soften Lorna's heart. She felt Him prompting her, *Go and whisper in your husband's ear that he doesn't need to worry about a place to live, that he can come back home.* Hard as it was, she obeyed. Carefully navigating all the machines and the tubes that were attached to him, she made her way to his side and whispered in his ear, "I want you to come home, honey. I love you. We will work it out."

Pascal recovered and did return home. A few days later, as he was sitting on the couch in the living room, Lorna went and knelt in front of him. "You know, honey," she said, "there have been so many hurtful things that have happened in our lives over the past years that I have lost trust in you. But I want you to know that I forgive you."

Soon after that day, in response to the grace he had received from Lorna, Pascal surrendered his life to Christ. The transformation that followed was dramatic—nothing short of miraculous. Pascal immediately, remarkably, lost his urge to drink, and "total restoration, total recovery" came to their home. Lorna recalls that "we started having family meetings, prayer meetings. There were flowers, postcards, and quiet candlelight suppers . . . a host of things that many people never experience in a marriage."

Four months later, at about four o'clock on a Tuesday morning, Pascal woke Lorna up. "Lorna," he said tenderly, "a man should love his wife with all his heart, with all his soul, and with all his mind, as God has loved us. I want to tell you at this moment that I love you that way."

Those were the last words Lorna ever heard from her husband. A few hours later, while she was at work, he had another massive heart attack and went to be with the Lord. And though she still misses him, she thanks the Lord every day for His grace in her life and in her marriage. She says,

> I don't know where I would be today without it. My husband
> probably would have died some place, and there would have
> been no forgiveness. The children would not have known
> what it was to have the love and leadership of a husband and
> father in the home. They experienced this in such a profound
> manner that today we can rejoice as a family and remember
> the wonderful times the Lord gave us for those four months.

God created marriage to tell the Story of His amazing grace
and covenant love. Not surprisingly, the enemy works hard to
keep that from happening. But the Holy Spirit is able to infuse
hope, help, and healing into the life of any person who is willing
to let Him write (or re-write) the story of his or her marriage.

Of course, no amount of effort, prayer, or faith can guarantee
that a marriage will be miraculously restored. One spouse cannot
control the choices of another. But God's love and mercy hold
firm and steady regardless of the outcome. And a husband or
wife who is willing to trust and obey God even in the midst of a
difficult marriage or an unwanted divorce will have the joy of
drawing close to Christ, receiving His grace, and reflecting the
gospel Story of His redeeming love.

*How have you found God to be faithful
in unexpected or difficult chapters of your life?*
Share your story *on your favorite social media platform.*
#TrustGodToWriteYourStory

CHAPTER 5

You Can Trust God When You Long for a Mate

*God never denies us our heart's desire
except to give us something better.*

ELISABETH ELLIOT

*B*ack in 1968, when I (Robert) was a college student, a song called "One," penned by Harry Nilsson, was released by the Australian band Three Dog Night. The lyrics famously proclaimed that the number one is "the loneliest number" a person can ever experience.

That song neared the top of the charts in its day and continued to strike a chord through the decades, covered by a number of artists and featured in the soundtracks of quite a few well-known movies and TV shows. Why did it continue to show up? We think it's because it expresses a deep-down sentiment that is familiar to many—including a number of our dear friends who wait for God to fulfill their dream for a mate.

The late missionary, author, and speaker Elisabeth Elliot once described suffering as "having what you don't want or wanting what you don't have."[1]

The people whose stories we shared in the last chapter know what it is to have what they don't want—pain and dysfunction in their marriage, the most intimate human relationship. That kind of suffering may be part of your story.

Or you may be suffering in a different way—longing for something God has not chosen to give you—the gift of marriage. Perhaps you've never been married. Or maybe you're single again, having lost a mate through death or divorce.

It's tempting for those in an unhappy marriage to think that if they didn't have their particular mate, they would be better off . . . while those who long for marriage sometimes feel they would be fulfilled if only they did have a mate.

From earliest childhood we've been conditioned through pop culture and plenty of other influences to believe that there's a prince for every princess and that love, romance, and marriage equal "happily ever after." Just think of all those Disney movies and romantic comedies that portray marriage as the ultimate goal and singleness as a fate from which to be rescued.

When real life doesn't prove to be a fairy tale or a romantic comedy, the burden of unmet hopes and expectations can be overwhelming. Over the years, many women have shared with me (Nancy) their struggle with trusting God when it comes to their love life:

- "I'm fifty-two, never married. God knows what's best for me? I'm barely surviving under the crushing weight of loneliness. I am weary from my anger and bitterness. All my friends, younger siblings and atheist friend included, have been happily married for decades and have grown children. My godly mother prayed for decades for me to find a Christian man. She died never seeing her prayer answered. I don't understand."

- "I want to believe God has a plan for me, and that's why I am still single. But I find it hard to look forward to the future. I don't understand why so many are blessed with families and husbands. Does God love these women more?"

Elisabeth Elliot herself experienced seasons of marriage interspersed with spells of singleness.[2] She was widowed the first time at the age of twenty-nine, after just twenty-seven months of marriage, when her husband Jim was brutally speared to death while serving Christ in Ecuador. Elisabeth was left with a ten-month-old baby girl. Nearly three years later, Elisabeth returned with her towheaded little girl to the very village in the foothills of the Andes (in the Amazon rainforest) where her husband was murdered to share the Story of God's love and forgiveness with the Huaorani people. She stayed with the Huaorani two years, then continued as a missionary to another tribe before returning to the United States.

After nine years as a widow and a single mother, Elisabeth married again, only to have her second husband die of cancer four years into their marriage. After four more years she married her third husband, who would survive her. During all of her eventful life, she learned what it meant to trust God with the unexplainable when what she received was not what she had asked or hoped for.

We are blessed to have many friends whose lives, like Elisabeth, beautifully demonstrate what it means to trust God in a prolonged season of singleness. Not without testing and struggle at times, but in a way that points to the goodness and love of our Father. In the pages to come we will share three snapshots from their journeys.[3]

From the time she was a young girl, *"Cassandra"* dreamed of someday being married. And once she graduated from college, she assumed that would be the next step, as was the case with many of her friends. But the years wore on, and Cassandra has not yet married.

Now in her fifties, Cassandra sometimes finds it hard to find things to talk about at family gatherings or church functions . . . no husband, no children. Seeing nieces and nephews marry and have children has also been difficult at times. While she is genuinely happy for them, that kind of news can cause an ache in her heart—the feeling of "I missed out" or "I've been left behind."

For her, the challenges of singleness and unfulfilled longings have often centered on the anxiety of being alone, the feeling of missing out or being left behind, and nagging self-image questions that lead her to wonder, *Is there something wrong with me?* (For the record, she is an amazing, lovely, grace-filled woman.)

Cassandra has always longed for a godly man to pursue her, but not much of that has happened so far. She has briefly dated a few men who asked her out, but they didn't appear to be particularly interested in spiritual matters—a

> How does Cassandra deal with the unfulfilled longings still in her heart? She chooses to look for the good in each day rather than focusing on what she thinks she is missing out on. "I've been given today to prove God is sufficient," she says. And He is.

nonnegotiable for Cassandra. When the relationships ended, friends and family questioned whether she was being too picky. But in each case the caution she felt was confirmed, and she is grateful the Lord protected her from getting involved with or marrying someone who did not share her love for Christ.

So how does Cassandra deal with the unfulfilled longings still in her heart? "'By counseling my heart according to God's Word,' seems like the perfect Sunday school answer," she says. "But it's true; it works." Cassandra has learned through the years that talking to God when she's lonely, overwhelmed, jealous, or fearful brings her comfort and direction.

She chooses to look for the good in each day rather than focusing on what she thinks she is missing out on. "I've been given today to prove God is sufficient," she says. And He is.

We have been touched to see this woman pour herself out on behalf of her family, friends, and others. She is a bright light wherever God places her, a steadfast source of encouragement to us and so many others. And she keeps her gaze fixed on Christ and on the eternity she will spend as His bride.

Postscript: As this book was getting ready to go to press, a godly widower initiated a relationship with Cassandra. We have rejoiced with her as love has been awakened in her heart. It appears that the Lord is in the process of fulfilling her long-time desire to be married—a gift that she is thrilled about, but that she also knows will never be as precious as the eternal, all-surpassing gift of His love. How sweet it is to watch as this dear friend continues to trust God to write her story.

Just two years apart in age, **Bethany Baird (now Beal)** and her older sister, Kristen, were the best of friends. But when Kristen announced her engagement to Zack, Bethany knew that the dynamic in their relationship was going to shift. Soon Kristen would be a married woman, and Bethany would still be single.

But Bethany wasn't really worried. She assumed that wedding bells would be coming her way within the next year or two. Instead, she would be single for the next seven years.

During that time most of her friends got married and started having babies. She attended dozens of weddings, purchased bridesmaid dresses for many of them, and hosted multiple wedding and baby showers—all as a single woman—wondering if her own big day would ever come. It felt to her as if others' lives were moving forward and she was being left behind.

Facing her unmet romantic expectations was difficult for Bethany. She didn't like the thought of not being married. She didn't want to attend singles groups, go on countless dates, or have to come up with escorts for all those weddings. She wanted a man of her own. And she wanted him sooner rather than later.

Looking back now, however, Bethany believes that this season of singleness was part of God's perfect and good plan for her life, even though that plan didn't place her at the wedding altar as soon as she had hoped.

During those years, Bethany was impacted by a well-timed observation she read in Nancy's book called *Choosing Gratitude*:

> I have learned that in every circumstance that comes my way, I can choose to respond in one of two ways: I can *whine* or I can *worship*.[4]

Bethany took Nancy's advice to heart and it changed her mindset—especially during "wedding season" in spring and early summer. The more she said no to whining and the more she focused on worshiping Christ, the more she was able to rejoice with others when God blessed them with good gifts.

But trusting God with her own love story was still not always easy for Bethany. She could trust Him for other people's journeys, and she could see that He was directing and working in their lives. But she frequently questioned His work in her own life. Finally, she realized she needed to get serious about learning how to trust God. She searched the Scriptures and realized that God truly is the same yesterday, today, and for all of eternity. This God, who has always been faithful to His children, really can be trusted with every detail of our lives, now and forever.

This new perspective was a huge game changer for Bethany. It freed her to flourish during those years of singleness and to enjoy all that God intended for her in that season. Instead of waiting around for a husband, she started pouring her heart and time into serving the Lord and others. First, she began mentoring and discipling young women and got serious about serving in her church. Then, she and Kristen cofounded GirlDefined Ministries and began coauthoring books. As she took her eyes off her own needs and focused more on the needs of others, as she focused on using her life to serve Christ, she found true contentment and satisfaction as a single woman.

And then, in God's Providence, God brought a man into Bethany's life who loves her dearly—and loves the Lord even more. What a joy it was for me (Nancy) to watch their sweet journey and to join thousands of others in watching the live stream of her wedding to David Beal one month after her thirtieth birthday.

Before Bethany married, she shared her heart on surviving the wedding season as a single woman in a blog post for Revive Our Hearts. She concluded:

> Whether you're nineteen, twenty-five, or thirty-nine, it's
> possible to thrive during wedding season. Let's put on those
> party dresses, buy those wedding gifts, sign those guest
> books, and eat that cake with joy for our marrying friends
> and with faith in God's plan.[5]

Today Bethany gratefully embraces the gift of marriage, trusting God for whatever His plan is for her in the days ahead—something she first learned when trusting Him to write her story when she was still single.

***

"Katie" is one of nine siblings, five of whom are married. So far she has thirteen nieces and nephews.

Though she is in her midthirties, Katie told us that at times she has felt like an immature teen, praying things like, "You let all Your other kids date! Why won't You let me?" But in her heart she knows that her life is in God's hand, and if He wants to give her a husband someday, He can certainly bring that about. "He has His reasons," she said. "He can *absolutely* be trusted to write our stories."

> "God, I know You could bring a husband to me. But even if You don't, even if singleness is for the rest of my life here on earth, I still trust You. I'm still in. You're still worthy." (Katie)

She confessed that at times she's been tempted to scrap it all and just date the next cute guy that chats her up at Starbucks. But her heart and imagination have been captured by something far more beautiful. "The great yes to Jesus always draws me back," she said with her characteristic warmth and shining countenance. And then she quoted the words of John 6:68 as her own: "Lord, to whom shall we go? You have the words of eternal life."

For several years, Katie worked as a graphic designer in a nonprofit organization. It was during that season that she came to experience the reality of the gospel and the love of Christ in a whole new way. He radically changed her desires and aspirations and gave her a heart to minister to those who are marginalized and in desperate need of His love and grace. Finally, she stepped out in faith, raised her own financial support, and moved to a country that is closed to the gospel, where she now serves among an unreached people group, seeking to love and point others to Christ.

> We cannot promise that God will change your situation, at least not yet. But we can assure you that you are loved—deeply loved, with the steadfast love of the Lord, a love that never fails.

Signing a four-year-plus commitment in a foreign country was a fresh test. Doing the math, she realized that she may well be out of the childbearing years before she returns to the States.

> This was the first time I remember wondering, "God, are You asking lifelong singleness of me?" and I grieved. But years of experiencing His faithfulness in big and small dreams let me say, "God, I know You could bring a husband to me on the mission field, but even if You don't, even if singleness is for the rest of my life here on earth, I still trust You. I'm still in. You're still worthy."

I (Nancy) long for each of my unmarried friends to fully embrace the conviction that has proved to be an anchor for Cassandra, Bethany, and Katie's hearts in their season of prolonged singleness, as it was in mine: God is good, and You can trust Him to write your story.

Well, that's easy for you to say, you may be thinking. *God gave you a husband. But He hasn't given me one!*

Here's what I know. During my fifty-seven years as a single woman, I had my times of loneliness and longing for deeper companionship. But I also experienced sweet contentment, joy, and fruitfulness as I learned to trust God to direct my life, meet my needs, and walk with me through the challenges of that season. And now that I am married, I know that Christ—not my husband, precious as he is—is my highest good, my unfailing hope, and that I can trust Him with whatever this chapter of my life may hold.

For thirteen years (beginning at age sixty-three), Elisabeth Elliot hosted *Gateway to Joy,* a daily syndicated radio program. She opened each broadcast with the same, familiar words:

> *"You are loved with an everlasting love."*
> *That's what the Bible says.*
> *"And underneath are the everlasting arms."*
> *This is your friend, Elisabeth Elliot. . . .*

These words provided perspective and solace for her listeners, married and single alike.

You may have unfulfilled longings for a mate—or find yourself in a troubled marriage where you feel alone. We cannot promise that God will change your situation, at least not yet. But we can assure you that you are loved—deeply loved, with the steadfast love of the Lord, a love that never fails.

Perhaps you long to be held by someone who truly cares for you and is committed to your well-being. The everlasting arms of God are supporting and surrounding you, carrying and caring for you.

Do you long for a friend who knows and desires you? In Christ, you have the dearest Friend a soul could have, one who walks with you today and will be yours for all of eternity.

How have you found God to be faithful
in unexpected or difficult chapters of your life?
Share your story *on your favorite social media platform.*
#TrustGodToWriteYourStory

CHAPTER 6

You Can Trust God When You're Pressed Financially

*God is a wise Father
who sometimes refuses what you want
to give you what you need.*

H.B. CHARLES JR.

On Thursday, February 28, 1992, a phone call rang through the switchboard (remember those?) at the publishing company I (Robert) owned with my business partner, Michael Hyatt. The call was from a friend . . . who also happened to be the CEO of a company to which our business was in debt.

"I don't want to do what I'm about to do," he said haltingly. "But I'm a man under authority, and I have no choice."

My heart jumped. This didn't sound like it was going to be a happy conversation.

It wasn't. The next words I heard were, "I'm calling your note."

That was it. His company was a subsidiary of a larger company, and he had been given "orders from headquarters" to pull the plug on the business Mike and I had started five years earlier.

After a short silence I spoke. "Are you sure?"

"Yes."

Hoping for some time to think and process, I asked if he and I could speak again the following morning to absolutely confirm this news. I wanted to be certain it was really happening before we informed our team. He agreed and promised to speak with his superiors one more time.

Walking over to my office door, I closed it. Then I sat down on the floor next to my desk and wept. The dream that was our business was finished. And since everything I owned was leveraged against this business, I now faced the possibility of losing it all along with suffering the insecurity and embarrassment of not being able to make ends meet.

I didn't want to trust God in that moment. I didn't want to believe that He knew what was best. What I wanted was pity—and perhaps even revenge. We hadn't managed our business perfectly, but we didn't deserve this.

> In the midst of it all, we saw God provide for us and for our staff in some remarkable ways. (Robert)

Dazed, I got up and walked down the hall to Mike's office. Without knocking I opened the door, stepped in, and delivered the news. He stood up spontaneously as if rising in reverence when a funeral procession passes. This was news that could not be received sitting down.

After that we spent a long time together, trying to figure out how to respond. At first there was anger. Then disbelief. Then resignation. And finally, through tears, we dared to trust God— to believe that He was writing a story. At the time, of course, we could not understand why the plot was unfolding this way.

But although we could not imagine how it would all end, we knew ultimately it would be good—because God is good and all His ways are good.

That call came on my forty-fourth birthday. The adult Sunday school class I taught each week had given me a gift card to a nice downtown restaurant. So my wife, Bobbie, and I went out for the evening to celebrate my birthday—and to talk about the news I had just received.

Never once—that night, or in the difficult months that followed—did Bobbie belittle or berate me. I was defenseless, and she could easily have crushed my spirit. She was well aware that Mike and I had poured everything we had into this business. But she never said, "I told you so" or "You've taken all of our money and squandered it." Bobbie's support and encouragement in that season was a huge gift and a channel of God's grace to this hurting man.

The next morning I went to the office. After confirming with the CEO that the situation had not changed, Mike and I called our team together and explained that we were closing our business, and they were all officially unemployed. Then we set about doing what we had to do to get through the coming months.

Unable to handle our mortgage, Bobbie and I sold our large, lovely dream home and moved into a rental house. Because we would not be able to make the payments, we returned our second car to the dealer. We pulled our older daughter out of private school and seriously streamlined the budget for her upcoming wedding.

And as impossible and unnatural as it felt, in the days that followed, Mike and I remembered and embraced God's faithfulness. We did our best to comply graciously with the demands of the company that had closed us down. Our staff cleaned out their desks and went to the unemployment office. In just a few days, the company sent their representatives with a truck to take our furniture and computers. Through it all, we tried to lean hard into what we knew to be true of Him and His ways, even though, at the time, both the present and the future looked bleak.

The whole experience was incredibly humbling. Self-doubt and fear sometimes wrapped themselves around me like a soaking wet blanket. But in the midst of it all, we saw God provide for us and for our staff in some remarkable ways.

We watched our families and the body of Christ rally to encourage and help. One of our staff, for example, was a single mom. When word got out that she had lost her job, friends collected money and bought clothes for her preteen daughter. One day, Bobbie and I got home and discovered several bags of groceries at the back door, left there by an anonymous friend who knew our need and wanted to help out. One of my brothers called me frequently to check in and make sure we were okay, taking our relationship to a new level.

And in God's Providence, the loss proved to be a catalyst for redirecting my life vocationally. Mike and I started a new company—a literary representation agency. Six years later I bought him out and he returned to corporate life, where he ultimately rose to become the CEO of the company and then went on to become a bestselling author and productivity guru.

> I doubt that I ever would have written a word had it not been for the unexpected, unwanted call I received on my forty-fourth birthday. It all happened in His perfect time, according to His trustworthy script. (Robert)

As for me, being a literary agent has been a true gift from the Lord. In addition to providing for my family through this (debt-free!) business, He has given me the privilege of coming alongside hundreds of authors to help turn the messages in their hearts into published books. Further, the agency business created margin in my schedule to pursue other dreams and ministry endeavors.

In 1996, I wrote my first of now more than twenty books, sharing encouragement and insights for dads of daughters. I seriously doubt that I ever would have written a word had it not been for the unexpected, unwanted call I received on my forty-fourth birthday. It all happened in His perfect time, according to His trustworthy script.

Even now, nearly thirty years later, my eyes well up with tears thinking about how painful this whole experience was. But I'm also overwhelmed by how faithful and good my heavenly Father has been and how thankful I am for His leadership in my life. In retrospect, knowing what I know now (and realizing there is much I do not yet know), I would not choose to rewrite a single scene of this story.

The story of my (Nancy's) family also includes a chapter on major financial loss. It took place during my sophomore year in high school. As the Lord would have it, that is the year I took World Cultures, a class taught by Roy Parmelee. "Coach Parm," as he was affectionately known, also coached boys' basketball. Most importantly, he understood and taught history from a Christian worldview.

As we studied the rise and fall of nations, two world wars, key figures who influenced their eras, and belief systems that shaped the course of history, my heart became deeply grounded in the conviction that the sovereign God of the universe reigns over both the big events of world history and the most minute details of His creation.

This was not a new theological concept to me, having grown up saturated in Scripture at home, church, and in Christian school. But now I was seeing God's sovereignty being worked out in the panorama of world history, and the sight was stunning to my young heart. Never again would I see this world—or my world—with the same eyes. I knew without a doubt that "this is my Father's world."

During that same school year, through a series of difficult circumstances my family walked through, I would also experience firsthand the comfort, calm, and confidence that come from knowing that heaven rules and that a wise, good, sovereign God is intimately involved in every chapter of our lives.

Throughout that entire year, my dad's business was under fierce attack. He had come up with the idea of selling health and life insurance directly to consumers, bypassing agents. But though direct marketing of insurance is now common, back in the 1970s it was frowned upon by the industry. The regulatory body in the State of Pennsylvania did everything they could to shut his business down, and for a while it looked like they might succeed. My dad ultimately prevailed, but not before his adversaries managed to nearly decimate both his business and his personal net worth.

Through it all, Art DeMoss never panicked. He had taught us that everything we have comes from and belongs to God, that He is the source of every material blessing—not a business, not some kind of investment, not the stock market, not a healthy economy. He recognized that we do not deserve any good gifts from God and that, as the Owner of everything, God has the right not only to give, but also to take away, if that is what pleases Him.

This trial was not the first time my dad had experienced the need to trust God in relation to his finances. As a kid I remember hearing him share that when he first became a believer in 1950, two weeks before his twenty-fifth birthday, he was tens of thousands of dollars in debt. (That's equivalent to hundreds of thousands in today's dollars.) And this had happened in spite of the fact that he was accustomed to working seven days and five nights a week at his start-up business.

Like many entrepreneurs, Dad had the notion that he was indispensable to his company and that if he left for a day or two he would return to find everything gone. So he did his best not to leave! If he had to be gone for even for a few hours, he would call the office frequently to make sure everything was all right. But something changed once he chose to hand over his life to God. As he later explained it:

> The Lord saved me and promised to meet all my needs. . . .
> I can testify to the glory of God that, in spite of my frequent
> unfaithfulness, He has always been more than faithful. He
> first took me out of debt shortly after my conversion. . . . I did
> not need to work night and day and Sundays as in the past.
> All I had to do was put God first.[1]

For the rest of his life, Art DeMoss did put God first. But that didn't mean God spared him from heartaches and hardships.

The business reversal he went through when I was in tenth grade was just one of multiple pressures our family faced in that season. During the previous year, my mother had experienced serious complications prior to giving birth to my youngest sister, number seven in our family.

Nine months later, the night before a new school year began, a fire broke out in our home in the middle of the night, with twelve people sleeping inside. Miraculously all were saved, but the house suffered major damage. We were briefly farmed out to friends' homes until another house became available for us.

Then, at the end of that same school year, my mother underwent surgery to remove a life-threatening brain tumor that had been growing undiagnosed for a decade. Mercifully she recovered, though with permanent equilibrium issues and complete loss of hearing in one ear.

As I watched my dad weather that period of relentless storms, I saw a man who, amazingly, was at peace. While wave upon wave pounded our family, his heart was steadfast. Through one adversity after another, even before knowing the outcome, he consistently modeled what it meant to offer a sacrifice of praise.

Tethered to the sovereignty and Providence of God, he was able to be as grateful and serene in times of great loss as he had been in times of great gain.

The example of my parents in this season, along with that world cultures class with Coach Parm, gave me a yearlong course in Theology 101. What I gained from those lessons was not dry dogma encased in some dead textbook, but a living, pulsating,

> As I watched my dad weather that period of relentless storms, I saw a man who, amazingly, was at peace. While wave upon wave pounded our family, his heart was steadfast, tethered to the sovereignty and Providence of God. (Nancy)

vibrant faith in the God who reigns over every part and particle of His creation, tenderly cares for His own, and is always accomplishing His eternal redemptive purposes in this world.

Both Robert and my dad experienced what it is to trust God in the face of cataclysmic financial loss. My long-time colleague **Mike Neises** has another kind of story. For more than twenty years, he and his wife, **Chris,** have trusted God to supply their "daily bread" in a different way than most.

While in his forties, as a fairly young believer, and having worked his way up to a responsible management position in a family-owned company in northern Indiana, Mike began to feel restless, wanting to be more involved in ministry. He and Chris started praying, "Lord, we're open to whatever You may have for us to do."

Over the next couple of years, the Lord orchestrated a series of circumstances that ultimately resulted in Mike's leaving his "secure" job in the corporate world to take a position in a ministry where we served together for twenty-two years. This would involve a significant pay cut—not until his seventeenth year in the ministry would his W-2 income exceed his highest W-2 in the job he had left. In addition, he and Chris also became responsible to raise a portion of their monthly support, as many missionaries do.

At the time they began this process, they had three teenage kids. When they first shared their decision with their friends and family (many of whom were not believers), some thought they were being foolish and that it was irresponsible to jeopardize a good job. Some wondered aloud how they would provide for their family.

About two years into the support-raising process, while still working at his industry job, Mike hit a wall. Deeply discouraged and making minimal progress, he met with his pastor to seek counsel: "Do we keep going?"

The pastor's response sustained him in that dark period: "God is seldom early but never late."

Soon after that conversation Mike's company was sold, and changes made by the new management team gave Mike the push he needed to make the break, step out in faith, and transition to his new role in our ministry, where he has been an incredible servant and asset to our leadership team.

Not long after that, the Lord confirmed His commitment to provide for this family in an amazing and faith-building way. Their oldest child, Brian, had spent a gap year after high school serving in a mission hospital in Bangladesh. He was just getting ready to go to college when Mike joined our ministry.

Brian had applied to just one school, a Christian liberal arts college he felt strongly led to attend, to prepare for teaching internationally. With Mike's reduced income, that school now seemed out of the question financially. But a month before school was to start, the college called and informed Chris that a new scholarship had just been established for someone who wanted to be a teacher, and they asked for permission to submit Brian's name for consideration.

Brian had not applied for the scholarship. He hadn't even known it existed. But of course the family gave permission for him to be considered. And a week later Chris received another call, letting her know that her son had been the one selected to receive this scholarship. Full tuition. All four years of college. Paid in full.

When Chris called Mike to relay the news, Mike says, "I sat in my office, weeping on the phone with Chris as we praised God for this provision, right at the beginning of this new journey of faith."

God's provision for Mike and his family over these years has not always been quite so dramatic, but it has always been there when they needed it. At one point, for instance, knowing that they would not have discretionary funds to hire people to do things around the house and not being particularly handy or mechanically inclined, Mike laid the situation before God. "Lord," he prayed, "I'm willing to try to fix anything, but I need You to show me how, lead me to the right resources, help me learn." (This was before there were YouTube videos available on every project.)

After that, whenever a need arose, whether it involved replacing tires, dealing with broken garage doors, fixing electrical problems or plumbing breaks, refinishing floors, or renovating a kitchen, God brought people along to help or directed Mike to how-to books at the library, making it possible for his family to live within their means.

> Isn't that the point of each of our stories? That we would trust Him— whether having much or little of this world's goods— in such a way that those around us would exclaim, "Look at their God! What a good, faithful Provider He is!"

The provision continued as time went on. Mike and Chris's other two children were also able to graduate from Christian colleges with minimal debt. And later, when the children were grown, the Lord provided a way for Chris to get her nursing degree, supplying another source of income for the family.

Chris shared with us the impact this journey has had on their children, now grown with families of their own. She observed that "all three are very frugal, not always looking for the next thing to buy; they make do and are happy with what they have."

Now, in their late sixties, Mike and Chris are facing uncharted territory in terms of retirement. As they have done for all these years, they are lifting their eyes up to their heavenly Father, asking for and trusting in His provision. "We're able to rest, knowing that He has provided before and that the future is in His hands."

When we asked to talk with Mike and Chris for this book, they said, "We don't feel our story is remarkable. In fact, it seems pretty ordinary when you do things one day at a time."

Their final takeaway: "Our story says a lot about our God."

And isn't that the point of each of our stories? That we would trust Him—whether abounding or abased, having much or little of this world's goods—in such a way that those around us would exclaim, "Look at their God! What a good, faithful Provider He is. Isn't He amazing!"

How have you found God to be faithful
in unexpected or difficult chapters of your life?
Share your story *on your favorite social media platform.*
#TrustGodToWriteYourStory

CHAPTER 7

Redeemed

Naomi and Ruth's Story

How things appear to us and
how they actually are are rarely the same.
Sometimes it looks and feels like
the Almighty is dealing "very bitterly" with us
when all the while he is doing us and many others
more good than we could have imagined.

JON BLOOM

The era of the Old Testament judges was not a pretty one. Deeply rooted spiritual and moral rot ate away at the soul of the nation of Israel. God's chosen people rejected the One who had so powerfully rescued them from Egypt and had established them in the land of Canaan. Lawlessness and anarchy prevailed, unimaginable violence and unspeakable atrocities were committed with impunity, and people were afraid to leave their homes. Even those charged with safeguarding corporate worship were corrupt and easily bought.

Against this bleak backdrop we discover a lovely gem tucked away in the folds of Scripture, the story of two destitute women finding grace, redemption, and hope in the grain fields of a wealthy relative. Their story is remarkable on its own. But living as we do, in AD (*anno Domini,* "the year of our Lord"), rather than BC ("before Christ") as they did, we can see in a way they couldn't that they were a small part of a much bigger Story God was writing.

> This is a story of a wakeful, watchful God who knows when a sparrow falls to the ground, who knows the number of hairs on our head and the number of stars in the universe. A God who ordains and superintends all the details of our lives from the tiniest to the greatest. It is a story of divine Providence.

A small Jewish family made up the original cast of characters—a husband and father named Elimelech, a wife and mother called Naomi, and two sons, Mahlon and Chilion. In the first scene we find them cobbling their possessions together, fleeing a famine in their homeland, and finding refuge in the land of Moab. However, what they anticipated would be just a short sojourn turned into a long decade of compounded grief in a foreign land, far eclipsing the misery they had left behind in Israel.

First Elimelech died. In time, Mahlon and Chilion married local women, Orpah and Ruth, bringing new daughters-in-law and a measure of consolation to the widow Naomi. But then, improbably, the widow's sons also died, leaving behind two more widows.

When news reached these three that the famine in Naomi's homeland had finally ended, the older widow announced to her two daughters-in-law that she was going home. She urged them to stay with their own people in Moab and find new husbands to provide for them.

The scene was a tearful one. The three women had grown fond of each other, and they knew this goodbye would be forever. Finally Orpah turned to follow Naomi's advice.

But Ruth refused to leave Naomi. Clinging to Naomi, she promised her lifelong love and loyalty with these unforgettable words: "Where you go I will go, and where you lodge I will lodge. Your people shall be my people, and your God my God" (Ruth 1:16).

Naomi relented. With Ruth at her side, she turned her face toward home.

⁓

The unlikely narrative of catastrophic loss experienced by Ruth and Naomi could be the stuff of legend, but this story is true. It's also a breathtaking account of God's providential care, protection, and provision—and a reminder of His ability to overrule and redeem the losses occasioned by living in this broken, fallen world.

God used the loss of her husband and sons to get Naomi back to the town of Bethlehem, where the next chapter of her story would be written. In His kind Providence, God had gone before her and made provision, for she and Ruth "came to Bethlehem at the beginning of the barley harvest" (v. 22). And that was just the beginning. God was going to meet Naomi and Ruth's needs in ways they could not have envisioned.

After arriving and settling in Bethlehem, the younger widow, Ruth, set out looking for means to sustain their meager family. And the best option she could come up with was to become a gleaner—gathering up the bits of grain that were left in the field after the harvesters had done their work.

> So she set out and went and gleaned in the field after the reapers, and she happened to come to the part of the field belonging to Boaz, who was of the clan of Elimelech. (Ruth 2:3)

"She *happened* to come . . ." That's what it looked like from earth's perspective. The job search of this needy woman "happened" to lead her to the employment of a wealthy landowner, who just "happened" to be a relative of her deceased father-in-law . . . and who through an ancient legal provision would "happen" to become her husband and a lifelong provider for Ruth and Naomi.

A happy coincidence? Hardly.

A stroke of luck? Not at all.

This is a story of a wakeful, watchful God who knows when a sparrow falls to the ground, who knows the number of hairs on our head and the number of stars in the universe. A God who ordains and superintends all the details of our lives from the tiniest to the greatest.

It is a story of divine Providence.

God was at work writing the story of these two women. As every story does, this one had its unexpected twists and turns and moments in which the situation appeared to be unsolvable. By cultural norms, Ruth would have been spurned for her foreign ethnicity and shamed as a menial laborer. (Gleaners were on the low end of the economic food chain.) She had nothing to offer the successful Boaz.

But none of these painful realities could thwart God's master plan. This story was being skillfully crafted by the unseen hand of God.

In the midst of their misfortune, Naomi and Ruth demonstrated two very different views of God.

Naomi saw God as her Antagonist—the source of her misery:

> The hand of the LORD has gone out against me. . . . The Almighty has dealt very bitterly with me. I went away full, and the LORD has brought me back empty. . . . The LORD has testified against me and the Almighty has brought calamity upon me. (1:13, 20–21)

Ruth, on the other hand, saw God as her Protector—someone who could be trusted, even when she could not see or understand what He was doing. Boaz, who had heard of what she had done for Naomi, lauded her faith:

> A full reward be given you by the LORD . . . under whose wings you have come to take refuge! (2:12)

Ruth's trust was not in Boaz, generous and kind as he was. She looked beyond him to God Himself for safety and shelter, protection and provision. And He did not fail her—or her mother-in-law, Naomi.

Generations earlier, God had appointed a means for His people to assist needy family members. Known as the levirate law, it stipulated that if a Jew's land had been taken from him, a close male relative could buy back the land and restore it to the original owner. Likewise, if a married man died without children, the closest living male relative—called a kinsman-redeemer—had the duty to marry the widow, provide for her, bear offspring for the deceased, perpetuate the family name, and keep the inheritance and lands in the family.

Encouraged by her mother-in-law, who was familiar with

this law and knew that Boaz was a near kinsman to her deceased husband, Ruth approached Boaz and asked him to fulfill the role of a kinsman-redeemer on behalf of Elimelech's family. Being a noble man, Boaz readily agreed. However, he told Ruth, there was an even closer relative who, according to the levirate law, had the right and the responsibility to act as a redeemer for Elimelech's bereft family.

Boaz assured Ruth that he would deal with the situation and that one way or the other, she would have the protection of a kinsman-redeemer. And Naomi, who was finally learning to trust in the faithfulness of God and His masterful story-writing skill, counseled Ruth, "Wait, my daughter, until you know how the matter turns out; for the man will not rest until he has settled it today" (3:18 NASB).

> Who could have brought about this turn of events? Who but our great, redeeming God, who had orchestrated the whole string of circumstances from start to finish.

And what wise counsel this is for every moment of perplexity and every apparent dead end we face. *Wait until you see how things go. Christ—our heavenly Boaz—is at work, and He won't rest until He has resolved the matter in a way that will best meet your needs and showcase His glory.*

⌒

Boaz made his way to the city gate, where business deals were transacted, public announcements made, and legal matters settled. Before long, the kinsman he had spoken of came by. After gathering a group of city elders as witnesses, Boaz explained the situation to the man, saying in effect, "Naomi has returned from Moab. You're the nearest kinsman, so you have the right to redeem her family's land for her. I'm next in line after you. If you want to buy it, great. If not, just let me know, and I'll take care of it."

Without hesitating, the man responded, "You bet! I'll be glad to buy the land."

"Oh," added Boaz, "there's just one more thing. Ruth the Moabite is part of the package. When you redeem Elimelech's property, she'll become your wife. Any children she bears with you will have Elimelech's family name and all rights to his inheritance."

"Um, on second thought," the redeemer said, "I . . . uh . . . I just can't do it. That would wreck my own estate. You go ahead and redeem the land."

> Then Boaz said to the elders and all the people, "You are witnesses this day that I have bought from the hand of Naomi all that belonged to Elimelech and all that belonged to Chilion and to Mahlon. Also Ruth the Moabite, the widow of Mahlon, I have bought to be my wife, to perpetuate the name of the dead in his inheritance, that the name of the dead may not be cut off from among his brothers." (Ruth 4:9–10)

This was good news—wonderful news—not only for Ruth, but also for Naomi. All that belonged to Elimelech and all that belonged to his sons would now be cared for by the one who had paid the debt. Ruth, the widow, would now be a wife. Her husband's family name would be preserved, and Naomi would be rescued from poverty.

Who could have brought about this turn of events? Who but our great, redeeming God, who had orchestrated the whole string of circumstances from start to finish.

And there was more!

Once Ruth's marriage with Boaz was sealed, Ruth would bear a child named Obed. Obed would one day have a son named Jesse, and Jesse would have a son named David, who would become king of Israel and Judah. And fourteen generations later, one of David's descendants would have a son named Jesus—the Kinsman-Redeemer of all mankind!

Distressing as they were, the calamities experienced by Ruth and Naomi were not ultimate. At times these grieving women must have felt that their story was over. But their losses actually set the stage and provided a platform for God to continue writing His Story of redemption, as He does in all our losses and sorrows.

And in their generous benefactor and hero, Boaz, we are pointed to our ultimate Rescuer, Redeemer, and Husband.

CHAPTER 8

You Can Trust God When You Lose Your Health

God never wastes His children's pain.

AMY CARMICHAEL

ay back in the day, as a college student, I (Robert) was employed by a small contractor. (I don't mean my boss was a short man, just that I was his only employee.) Along with his many other skills, Richard Whitmer could lay bricks with the precision of a dentist. But he was too frugal to rent a front loader to lift pallets of bricks and heavy, wet mortar to the highest scaffolding. Besides, he didn't need that kind of equipment. He had me.

Another of my tasks in those days was wrestling large planks up onto the scaffolding so my boss could stand on them. These were long, cumbersome two-by-twelves. They were also old and scuffed, having been in my boss's inventory since the Truman administration at least. And in those days I never wore work gloves. So there I was carrying ancient, scuffed-up planks without gloves . . . you can finish the thought, can't you?

That's right. Getting splinters—some call them slivers, but

everyone calls them painful—was a regular thing for me.

"Ouch," I'd yelp and pull my hand back. Knowing what had just happened, Richard would reach for his pocketknife. I can still see him picking out the glistening blade with his thumbnail and "sterilizing" it by wiping it on his trousers. I can also remember the indescribable pain of Richard extracting the tiny particle of wood.

I never made a sound. No self-respecting laborer whines about anything. But believe me, I felt the pain.

If a little, temporary splinter brought me so much discomfort, what must the apostle Paul have felt about the "thorn" that constantly stabbed into his flesh? He wrote about it in 2 Corinthians 12: "To keep me from becoming conceited because of the surpassing greatness of the revelations, a thorn was given me in the flesh, a messenger of Satan to harass me" (v. 7).

We don't know exactly what Paul's thorn was, though there's been a lot of speculation over the years. Perhaps it was a chronic physical ailment or some other sort of unrelenting affliction. We do know that it was not extractable by someone's dirty pocketknife or by any other human means. And we know that it was no small problem for Paul. In fact, the Greek word translated "thorn" in this passage refers to a pointed piece of wood or a sharp stake on which someone might impale himself.[1] No small splinter, this.

Whether it's large or small, when you have a thorn, it's all you think about. It nags at you like a raspberry seed stuck between two teeth, and you feel you've got to get it removed as quickly as you can.

But what if you can't? And what if the thorn is a devastating—or terminal—illness? And, worse, what if it's not you who is suffering, but rather your child? Or your mate? What then?

Having walked with my late wife, Bobbie, through the journey of cancer, this issue of trusting God in illness is an especially personal one for me. On Valentine's Day 2012, Bobbie went in for surgery, her doctor having suspected the possibility of ovarian cancer. Our daughter Missy waited with me for the surgeon to come out and give us a report. The diagnosis was not what we had been hoping for: ovarian cancer, stage four. In that surreal moment, our lives were forever changed. And for the next thirty-two months our usual routines were upended with a labyrinth of appointments, tests, and treatments. It was certainly not a chapter we would have chosen for our story, but there is no doubt it was a chapter chosen for us by our wise, loving Father.

> Bobbie's illness was certainly not a chapter we would have chosen for our story, but there is no doubt it was a chapter chosen for us by our wise, loving Father.
> (Robert)

Almost every Sunday morning at church, we're reminded of the what-if-it's-your-mate question. Sitting across the aisle from us are **Ron and Jane Baker**. Ron is a retired physician and Jane is his faithful, almost-always-smiling, wife. For many years this couple served as medical missionaries in Sierra Leone, on the West African coast, where Ron grew up as a "missionary kid."

Ron and Jane usually arrive to the service a little later than we do, so the sight of him gently leading his bride of many decades to "their" seat is a familiar sight. Although Ron has probably always been a gentleman with Jane and taking her by the hand is not new, today Ron has no choice. Thirty-some years ago, Jane was diagnosed with a degenerative eye disease for which there is no cure and which usually progresses to blindness. Today

Jane is functionally blind. And the ever-pleasant Dr. Baker is her guide. Literally.

We asked Ron how he had avoided becoming resentful when the Lord wrote a different story than he would have chosen. He was quick to respond:

> The Lord has been so good to us and has used Jane's visual loss to help so many others that I don't remember the word *resentment* even crossing my mind. It's a privilege to serve her, especially when I think of how she supported and served the Lord (and me) all those years in Africa. I was in my element and back "home" where I had grown up, but it was a sacrifice for her to faithfully serve the Lord there.

Each time we witness this small procession of two saints on Sunday morning, we are touched with a fresh sense of what it means to trust God "in sickness and in health."

LeRoy and Kim Wagner have been dear friends of Nancy's for many years. For much of his life, LeRoy has been a bivocational pastor—in the pulpit on Sundays, behind the wheel of an eighteen-wheel rig during the week. Kim is an author, conference speaker, mother, and grandmother.

During the summer of 2017, the Wagners visited us in our home in Michigan. After dinner, as we sat and talked out on the deck, they updated us on some health issues LeRoy had been dealing with. At that point, a series of tests had not provided any answers for his persistent and worsening symptoms.

Fast forward one year.

We listened on a speakerphone as these friends described the past months of LeRoy's rapidly deteriorating health—endless rounds of doctor appointments, expensive tests with inconclusive results, and above all relentless, excruciating, mind-numbing pain.

Though an exact diagnosis had proved to be maddeningly elusive, apparently LeRoy was suffering from a rare neurological disease in which the immune system attacked the spinal cord. The myelin (protective) sheath around his spinal cord had been destroyed, causing shooting nerve pain and the feeling that one of his legs is on fire—"like the worst sunburn you've ever had"—day and night.

At times the constant burning and the leg spasms would intensify to the point that he could hardly catch a breath. Kim would lovingly whisper, "Breathe, LeRoy, breathe."

"I would never have thought that a person could live with this much pain," she told us.

LeRoy admitted to battling despair. He said he sometimes struggled to reconcile the fact that God is sovereign and good with what they had been walking through. "At the same time," he said, "God's sovereignty is the very thing that holds me and gives me an anchor—knowing that what He does is right, and that He has purpose and a plan for all of this."

What did LeRoy do in the face of the despair? "I cry a lot," he told us. "I think tears are good." He continued,

> Then I begin to think about the goodness of God and all the ways He has been so good to us. I counsel my heart, going over Scriptures that I know are true. Some days that exercise helps take my mind off the pain. Other days, the pain is so intense, all I can do is to cry out to Him.

The losses and the pain were real. But this couple wanted people to know that God's presence had been just as real, even though He hadn't given them a reprieve from their suffering or an explanation to get them through it. "We don't know how this is going to turn out. And we may never know why He does what He does, but we know that it will be good, and we keep trusting Him for that," said LeRoy.

"Are there times when you wish it was terminal?" Robert asked gently after hearing that our friend was living in perpetual physical anguish.

"I would welcome death," LeRoy replied. "Many times I've wanted the Lord to take me instead of continuing in this condition." Then he added,

> Sometimes I think it's easier to die for Christ than to live for Him in chronic, long-term pain. I would rather be in heaven. But I just want to please and honor Him. Nothing compares to what He went through for me.

Letting what he had just said sink into his own heart, LeRoy reflected, "I think that coming to trust the sufficiency of Christ is what long-term suffering is about in a believer's life."

Kim chimed in, affirming the Lord's faithfulness to them throughout this ordeal. Early on, when LeRoy started declining physically, she sensed the Lord reminding her that He would not abandon them. And He hadn't. "He has been so near," she said. "His love and His personal care have been demonstrated in so many ways."

"I think that coming to trust the sufficiency of Christ is what long-term suffering is about in a believer's life." (LeRoy Wagner)

LeRoy became emotional as he talked about how this whole experience had been both humbling and humiliating.

> Having eighty-five-year-old men open the door for me makes me feel so weak and inadequate. Then I recall the Lord's

promise to the apostle Paul about his thorn in the flesh: "My grace is sufficient for you, for My power is made perfect in weakness" (2 Cor. 12:9).

Then wistfully, thankfully, Kim mentioned a sweet blessing that had come out of this hardship:

> Because he is completely immobile in his chair so much of the time, we spend a lot of time praying together. This is such a joy. We didn't have as much time for that before.

As our conversation was wrapping up, LeRoy added a final thought. Though his voice was weak, his message came through loud and clear:

> When you're in great pain, with everything taken away, you can still pray, you can still worship, and you can still love others around you. Those three things cannot be taken away from you. Ever.

Powerful.

When we hung up from our call with these two dear friends, Nancy turned to me and expressed what we were both feeling:

> The Wagners are grieving being sidelined from ministry. But what they're doing now—enduring, praying, suffering—is the ministry God has for them in this season. And we've just been on the receiving end of that ministry.

As we've been writing this book, I (Nancy) have been following the pain-filled journey of blogger **Colleen Chao** through a steady stream of email updates she sent to friends and prayer supporters (how rich these have been!), as well as a series of personal email exchanges.[2]

Over the years Colleen has had to trust God with one

difficult chapter after another of her story. At the age of nineteen, "with a head full of dreams and the world on a string," Colleen was blindsided by her first bout with deep depression. Many painful episodes of anxiety and depression would follow in the next two decades, including panic attacks and long periods of crippling emotional pain.

A deep, unfulfilled longing for a husband was another chapter. Over the course of those years, she celebrated dozens of friends' weddings and babies while wading through her own silent grief.

> But it was here in the suffering of depression, anxiety, and long singleness that I learned more of God's goodness and power. He blessed me in surprising ways even as I watched my dreams turn to ash.

Being "free and single," Colleen eventually set out to serve the Lord in overseas ministry. But that dream, too, evaporated due to prolonged, debilitating physical ailments.

In her midthirties, Colleen finally met and married her long-awaited husband. Soon she gave birth to a beautiful baby boy. The joys of marriage and motherhood were dampened, though, when her son turned out to have multiple health issues of his own. She wrote, "It was one thing to endure illness myself; it was quite another to watch my small child suffer."

And yet a decade of illness—both her son's and her own— did a "grueling but glorious work" in Colleen's heart.

> I let go of my white-knuckled grip on life, and with each new suffering came a deeper, more joyful experience with Christ. I knew and loved Him more than ever. I experienced the power of His Spirit in me. And I was learning that true ministry came from walking closely with Him—even when it didn't look at all like I'd once dreamed it would.

In the summer of 2017, Colleen finally began experiencing some physical relief. It seemed that restored health was on the horizon. She and her husband were grateful and anticipating being able to return to more active ministry, free from the limitations of protracted sickness.

Just weeks into enjoying this newfound health, Colleen felt a lump in her right breast. She remembers vividly those first panicked moments of *What if . . .?* and *Why, Lord?*

When she was still awaiting a diagnosis, Colleen prayer-journaled and quieted herself before the Lord. Her heart was encouraged as she considered *His* perspective on this journey she was about to take:

> You have everything you need to walk through this uncertainty, Colleen. Cancer? No cancer? Good news? Bad news? I am orchestrating it all, I have seen the end from the beginning, and it is a good story. A glorious, captivating, praise-worthy, honorable, enduring story. My pen does not slip. I am the Great Storyteller, and you are safe within My embrace as I write your story.

It took fourteen weeks to confirm a diagnosis. Colleen had an aggressive form of breast cancer called invasive ductal carcinoma (IDC). For an entire week after learning the news, she sobbed her heart out. On the heels of a decade of chronic illness, "I was weary to the marrow of my soul and wondered if cancer might just be 'too much' for me."

Yet, as she continued to press in to Christ, Colleen came to realize that God was entrusting her with a "gift"—the gift of deeper fellowship with Him—wrapped as it was in packaging that looked anything but desirable.

> Last year God entrusted us with a weighty gift, a beautiful suffering. . . . And what a gift it has been. How do I begin to

describe the sweetness of Christ and His people in the midst of the carnage of cancer? . . .

Fifteen months later He's still outgiving us and proving that His ways are not our ways, His kingdom turns our expectations inside-out. He frees us from our small, short-sighted dreams and says, "Watch this." And my jaw drops open at the miracles He works when we simply say, "I trust You. No matter what."

From our vantage point, it's no small miracle to witness the heart of a woman who has endured endless appointments, tests, surgeries, and treatments, and can still lift her eyes to the Father and say, "I trust You. Regardless of what gifts You choose for me." Sweet fruit indeed.

> It's no small miracle to witness the heart of a woman who has endured endless appointments, tests, surgeries, and treatments, and can still lift her eyes to the Father and say, "I trust You. Regardless of what gifts You choose for me."

As we've seen, it's hard enough to trust God when the unwanted diagnosis has your name on it. But it can be even more difficult when it applies to those you love—when you have to trust Him to write *their* story.

An opinion piece written by one of Robert's clients, Joshua Rogers, and published by a major news outlet caught our eye as we were working on this chapter. The headline read, "My Baby Nephew Was Dying, and His Mother's Response Was Unforgettable."[3]

Joshua's nephew, Canaan, has Down syndrome. He also

suffers from a digestive disease that went misdiagnosed for some time and can be fatal in children like Canaan. One afternoon when he was just seven months old, the infant became totally listless, and his concerned parents, Caleb and Rebecca, took him to the emergency room. By the time they arrived, the child's body was in septic shock. Little Canaan was in serious condition.

Joshua recounts a moving scene that took place in the waiting area as the medical staff were frantically trying to stabilize baby Canaan:

> Right there in the emergency room, Rebecca did something remarkable: She got down on her knees and said, "God, I'm going to worship You right now. No matter what happens, You're still holy. You're still good."[4]

In that moment of frenzied activity surrounding her son's body, a mother in dire need prostrated herself in worship before her heavenly Father. She knew He could be trusted to write this story over which she had no control.

Canaan was placed on life support, and the doctors did not expect him to survive. Over the next several weeks, thousands of people around the world joined in pleading with God on behalf of the little boy. By God's mercy, his life was spared, but Canaan has continued to face major physical challenges. This family's journey has not been and likely will not be an easy one. But the family remains committed to trusting God for this little boy. As Joshua's article concluded:

> Only God can give us the grace to believe when it seems like there's no miracle to be found; but when He does, the result is truly miraculous. We can, like my sister-in-law, bow down in the darkness and declare, "God, I'm going to worship You right now. No matter what happens, You're still holy. You're still good."[5]

This kind of grace-enabled faith—especially in the midst of the blackest night—is simply stunning. When His children offer up such costly worship—as Rebecca did in that waiting room and as our friends Ron and Jane Baker, LeRoy and Kim Wagner, and Colleen Chao continue to do in their battle with chronic physical issues—His Story is proclaimed to those who might not otherwise ever have heard it. And heaven applauds as His loved ones on earth acknowledge that He is worthy to be praised.

No matter what.

How have you found God to be faithful
in unexpected or difficult chapters of your life?
Share your story *on your favorite social media platform.*
#TrustGodToWriteYourStory

CHAPTER 9

You Can Trust God When You've Been Sinned Against

God is working in the hearts of those who have
wronged us as well as in our hearts. . . .
The justice of God is far more sure and unerring,
for it is the justice of love.

ERIC LIDDELL

*T*he soreness in *"Winona's"*[1] soul found expression in page
after page of her journal. In the wake of the long-kept secret finally
coming to light—that she had been sexually abused for twelve years
by a man who had been influential in shaping her faith as a young
believer, a man she had trusted—a torrent of emotions burst forth.

> Now everyone knows. At least some version of knowing.
> But no one knows the feeling of his hand on my head or
> the feeling of panic when he was on top of me, determined
> to have his way with me, while I squirmed and pushed and
> reasoned and pleaded to avoid it.
> No one knows the tears and desperation and silence
> between me and God while I tried to reconcile the actions
> of this "man of God," my desire for them to not happen, my
> participation in them, and God's view of me. Most of my

117

> years as a Christian have been defined by that confusion . . .
> the panic of that hand on the back of my head, the loss of
> more than a decade of my choices, the still dead places of my
> heart that were killed by a "man of God" who convinced me
> that I was making him sin.

Having been tossed around from one irresponsible, neglectful, and abusive adult to another throughout her childhood and youth, Winona was not prepared to encounter more of the same among her newfound "family" when she came to faith in Christ as a young adult.

Our dear friend is still reeling from the pain of her predator's behavior. Still struggling to get her bearings, to make sense of what for years she assumed *she* had somehow caused, and to deal with the implications of an unrepentant predator who cannot (or will not) see his sin or acknowledge the damage it has caused, and who has experienced only minimal consequences compared to what she endured at his hands.

∽

Adam and Eve were not just the first humans. They were also the first humans to betray one another. Once their relationship with God was shattered through pride and disobedience, it wasn't long before their relationship with one another devolved into blame and accusations (see Gen. 3). How much time had elapsed since their honeymoon when they threw each other under the bus? And how was it that their firstborn son later became envious and enraged enough to murder his younger brother in cold blood?

Being sinned against (and sinning against others) has been part of the human story from those earliest days to our own day.

The ways people sin against others are almost limitless. You may have experienced financial betrayal—an addicted child stealing from you or a sibling cheating you out of an inheritance. Perhaps you know what it is to have been falsely accused and wrongfully fired from your job after years of faithful service. You may have become disillusioned by a pastor who abused his authority and left his flock wounded and floundering. Or you may have been slandered by a jealous friend and your reputation left in tatters.

Deception, sexual abuse, violence, oppression, systemic injustice—these and a thousand other ways that human beings sin against one another—are the poisonous, heartrending fruits of humankind's treachery against God.

Sometimes these sins hit our lives (or the lives of those we love) with the force of a wrecking ball. It may take us years to regain our equilibrium. In some cases, the perpetrator may never (in this life) be brought to justice or repentance. All of which may lead us to feel that someone other than God is writing our story and to wonder whether He really can be trusted in the face of such atrocities.

> This is not one of those stories where someone prays and trusts God and He neatly puts together all the broken pieces and hands it back with a lovely bow on top. In fact, most of our stories aren't like that. We still live in a broken, fallen world where sin makes messes and its consequences are sometimes felt for generations.

Yet as you will see in the stories that follow and as Scripture attests, our faithful, loving God has the power to redeem the unredeemable and to turn ashes to beauty, not just *in spite of* the injuries we have suffered, but actually *through* those very wounds.

◦⁓⊃

"Alexis" recalls as if it were yesterday the night she learned her husband had a pornography addiction.

> I can still picture that moment—sitting in our hotel room in my pink-heart PJs, holding a hot fudge sundae, my eyes fogged up, feeling woozy from head to toe.

By all appearances and even from their own perspective, *"Darryl"* and Alexis had a decent marriage. They both came from intact, churchgoing families where Christ was honored.

Within the first years of their marriage, they had four children, nicely spaced out with two years between each birth. "We were in 'young-married-with-lots-of-little-people' surviving mode," Alexis recalled. "But we thought we were doing fine, considering how busy our lives were."

One day Alexis spotted a notice about a Christian marriage weekend retreat at a nearby hotel. She decided that their marriage could use some inspiration . . . a little brushing up, so she asked Darryl if they could go. He agreed.

On Saturday morning of the retreat, one of the speakers spoke of the perils of pornography. After the evening session, Alexis and Darryl picked up some ice cream and took it back to their room. Now they were sitting on their bed, enjoying the late-night calories and some lively chatter.

"The guy talked about pornography today," Alexis said matter-of-factly. "Have you ever seen porn?"

Like a cloud slowly blocking the sun, a shadow passed over Darryl's countenance. "Yeah," he said. "A few times."

I'm not skinny enough. That is one of the first thoughts she recalls crossing her mind at that moment. It would be some time before she would come to understand and believe that this issue was not about her, though the impact on her would be profound.

Finding Darryl's answer anything but satisfactory, Alexis pressed and probed for more information. At that point, she knew very little about pornography. It just wasn't talked about much back then, so the whole thing was foreign to her. But over the next couple of hours, as Darryl confessed a long-term addiction to pornography, she realized just how clueless she had been. She sat there paralyzed as he described a pattern of lying, precious hours wasted in front of his computer, and perhaps most damaging to their relationship, the inability to "do real" after years of fueling his appetite for fantasy.

Darryl had never shared this secret with anyone, not even his closest buddies. Starting with his first exposure in middle school, pornography for him had been a means of coping and escape. Like drugs or alcohol, it was something he ran to when life got difficult. He had hoped that sex in marriage would fulfill all his hopes and dreams and take away the urge. But he had come to realize that not even marital intimacy could satisfy the deep cravings that sent him back to porn again and again. (He would realize later that he had been looking to both porn and his wife to take the place of God in his life.)

In the midst of this self-imposed prison, Darryl had tried to be engaged as a husband and father. "But," he admitted when he and Alexis told us their story, "when you have a sin like this in your life, you're in a constant battle with God. He is opposed to the proud and gives grace to the humble." [2] Darryl swallowed hard, his voice choking back tears. Even all those years later, this was still a hard and humbling part of their story.

For the first several years of his marriage, Darryl had been careful in his online searches, trying to avoid being detected by his wife or others. But eventually he had thrown caution to the wind, adopting a "who cares?" attitude. Looking back, he realizes that was the point at which this practice turned into a full-blown addiction.

During that first sleepless night in the hotel after Darryl's confession, still struggling to catch her breath, Alexis wrote her husband a letter expressing her dismay over what she had learned, but also her commitment to walk through this with him if he was willing. She wrote,

> When we got married, I said, "for better or worse," and this is worse . . . "in sickness or in health," and this is sickness.

But could she ever trust him again? There had been lots of lying, lots of betrayal, and she was painfully aware that getting their relationship back to a healthy place would be a struggle.

When they got home, repulsed by what she had learned, Alexis wanted to strip the sheets off her bed. She remembers making PB&J sandwiches for the kids while thinking, *My husband has been unfaithful to me!* She had to keep moving, carrying on with her daily life, while carrying this huge weight.

The weeks that followed were tough, especially for Alexis. Getting his secret out had been a freeing experience for Darryl. Through honesty, humility, and repentance, the burden he had been carrying all these years was being lifted off his shoulders. But now that load had been transferred to Alexis.

Darryl and Alexis contacted a Christian counselor, who listened carefully to their story. Darryl held nothing back, fully exposing his sin. And the counselor was honest with Darryl about the fallout: "This is an open wound right now, and it's going to leave a scar." To this day, Darryl deeply grieves the pain he caused his wife.

As the Lord continued to deal with Darryl and began to heal their marriage, however, Alexis found her own heart being exposed as well. "I was completely self-righteous. I thought I was

a pretty good girl and that Darryl's sin was way worse than anything I had ever done." Only gradually did she come to realize she
needed the gospel just as much as Darryl did.

Over and over again Darryl asked his wife to forgive him. And
though Alexis tried, she found it really difficult to let go of her
resentment. Then one day Alexis heard a pastor say that forgiveness involves the willingness to pay a debt owed by someone else,
and something clicked inside her. That night she said to Darryl,
"I forgive you; I'll pay the debt. My sin is no less ugly than yours,
and I need Jesus as much as you do." And from that point, she
believes, their journey turned a corner.

Now, years later, Alexis says tenderly. "If we hadn't gone
through this, we would have stayed in a mediocre marriage. Our
crisis brought a ton of pain out, but our relationship has become
so real."

Darryl agrees. "Alexis didn't really have my whole heart before. Now she does."

Alexis is honest about the ongoing challenges. "Sometimes
if Darryl is going on a trip, I can panic. Or the memory will gush
up—I'm human; I can't forget. That's when I cry out, 'Jesus, I
need You to help me forgive again.'"

And Darryl still battles temptation at times. He knows he will
always be vulnerable in this area where he gave the enemy so much
ground. But he has demonstrated genuine repentance by fully
embracing a lifestyle of accountability and walking in the light—
with his wife and with a group of men he meets with regularly.

Again and again, both Darryl and Alexis remind themselves
how much they need the gospel, how they need to keep their eyes
fixed on Christ. They realize that this journey is not just about them.

For a while Alexis felt as if none of her close friends could
identify with her experience. She felt isolated and alone, without

anyone to lean on. But "then they started coming out of the woodwork"—women who were facing similar challenges in their own marriages. Over the past couple of years, God has used both Darryl and Alexis to help others who are caught in this particular snare. They have seen God turn ashes to beauty in their marriage, and they know He can do the same for others.

"Lauren" made her way to my (Nancy's) side at the front of the auditorium after hearing me speak. Her heart was heavy: "I never imagined I would be a divorced pastor's wife in my sixties, struggling to make ends meet and find some sense of purpose for my life."

> We have a Savior who knows what it is to be sinned against through no fault of His own. Even as He was being sinned against in the most outrageous ways possible—unjustly accused, beaten, and put to death—Jesus kept trusting God to write His story.

As a young girl, Lauren attended church almost every time the doors were open. She sat on the front row and admired her pastor's wife. Lauren wanted to be just like that woman when she grew up. She met her husband, *"Eric,"* at church; they married and attended Bible college together. They had three children, planted two churches, and enjoyed serving the Lord together for many years.

When they reached midlife, their church board began having some disagreements with Eric, and he resigned. For the next year he went through a dark season, struggling with hurt, discouragement, and lack of direction and vision. What Lauren didn't realize was that during this time he was also hiding something.

One humid night in July, when the family was gathered downstairs to celebrate Lauren's birthday, Eric pulled her aside and said, "I can't do this anymore."

"What can't you do anymore?" Lauren replied.

"Be married," Eric responded evenly. Lauren's heart froze, then broke in a million pieces.

Eric told her he had reconnected online with an old college girlfriend and decided she would make him happy. He wanted a divorce. Lauren prayed, begged, pleaded with him to change his mind. But this was what he wanted and eventually she let him have his way. Their children were devastated, as were many friends who had known them for years.

Never in a million years would Lauren have imagined herself divorced. Yet, this is exactly where she landed after thirty-two years of marriage. To make ends meet, she had to sell her beautiful home and she struggled to find a job in a market that didn't value mother-pastor's-wife credentials.

This is not one of those stories where someone prays and trusts God and He neatly puts together all the broken pieces and hands it back with a lovely bow on top. In fact, most of our stories aren't like that. We still live in a broken, fallen world where sin makes messes and its consequences are sometimes felt for generations.

Some of those messes will not be cleaned up this side of eternity. In the meantime we walk by faith, trusting His presence and grace to sustain us each day in the here and now, and assured that in the end He will right all wrongs and vindicate those who are His own.

Eric's unfaithfulness has made Lauren's life really hard. There's no way around that. But she clings to her faithful Father, who has promised to be with her, meet her needs, and carry her each step of the way. Following our conversation, Lauren wrote to me:

> Daily I come before the Lord and lay my life at His feet. I choose to trust Him with my story in this stage of my life, though it has not turned out as I wished. Even in my loneliness and disappointment, He is there. And I trust Him.

While the details of these stories—and of your story and mine—are different, what is the same for all of us is that we have been and will be sinned against (and that we have sinned and will sin against others). Also the same for all of us is the fact that God is still intimately involved in our stories and can be trusted to order our lives.

So what does it mean to trust God to write your story when others have sinned against you—perhaps grievously, perhaps with no evidence of remorse or repentance?

It means

- trusting that He has purposes for you—as well as for others who are part of your story—and that those purposes will be fulfilled in spite of (or perhaps even through) the wrongdoing you have endured;

- trusting Him to protect and provide for you, though others have failed to do so;

- trusting that in His way and time, He will deal with your offenders;

- trusting Him to protect your heart from becoming bitter or holding hostage those who have sinned against you;

- trusting Him for grace to forgive what seems unforgivable;

- trusting Him—in His way and time—to redeem and over-rule the losses caused by those who have sinned against you;

- trusting that the Holy Spirit can turn the heart of your of-fender and bring him or her to repentance and to a right relationship with God.

All of these responses might understandably seem unattain-able and perhaps even ludicrous if it weren't for the fact that we have a Savior who knows what it is to be sinned against through no fault of His own.

First Peter tells us that "Christ also suffered once for sins, the righteous for the unright-eous, that he might bring us to God" (3:18). Though He was the object of unimaginable abuse, "he did not threaten, *but contin-ued entrusting himself to him who judges justly*" (2:23).

Do you see that? Even as He was being sinned against in the most outrageous ways pos-sible—unjustly accused, beaten, and put to death—Jesus kept trusting God to write His sto-ry. And what was the outcome? "By his wounds you have been healed. For you were straying like sheep, but have now returned to the Shepherd and Overseer of your souls" (2:24–25).

> Our faithful, loving God has the power to redeem the unredeemable and to turn ashes to beauty, not just *in spite of* the injuries we have suffered, but actually *through* those very wounds.

In Christ's willingness to bear the wounds we inflicted on

Him, we have been healed of the wounds inflicted on us by our own personal sin and by the sin of a fallen world, which pits one person against another. Through His trust in the Father, our hearts have been brought back to the Father. How amazing is that!

Even so, as we entrust ourselves to God in those circumstances where we have been sinned against, He may not only bring us healing, but may also use us to be instruments of healing and repentance to our offenders. Regardless of whether we ever live to see that fruit in this life, we know that the One who judges justly will one day right every wrong.

How have you found God to be faithful
in unexpected or difficult chapters of your life?
Share your story *on your favorite social media platform.*
#TrustGodToWriteYourStory

CHAPTER 10

Sent

Joseph's Story

Providence is wiser than you,
and you may be confident it has suited
all things better to your eternal good
than you could do had you been left
to your own option.

JOHN FLAVEL

The sleeping teen wakened to the rude jostling of one of
the Midianite traders holding him captive. With the dawning
of a new day, it was time to continue the journey to Egypt, where
his new owners would sell him as a slave . . . ideally at a profit,
a hefty margin north of the twenty shekels of silver they had paid
to take him off his brothers' hands.

As his head cleared and he looked around at the unfamiliar
scenery, Joseph became painfully aware that this was not one
of his infamous dreams. It was in fact a nightmare, one that
would not dissipate with morning wakefulness. He stood and

brushed the dust from his tunic.

A grueling two-hundred-mile journey lay before them. Mile after trudging mile, Joseph couldn't help contemplating the perilous fate that awaited him as a slave. This was not at all what he had expected—definitely not the life he had dreamed.

As the favored and second youngest son of eleven brothers, he had been singled out by his father, Jacob, and lavished with affection and gifts. Now, narrowly avoiding cold-blooded murder by his jealous siblings, Joseph had been sold to passing merchants as a commodity to be traded.

How could this adolescent possibly have understood that a good, wise, unseen God was writing a story? His story. How could Joseph have seen that these tragic events were not random acts but rather carefully scripted scenes in a great, eternal drama of redemption? Of course, he could not.

From his finite point of view, all Joseph could have known for sure was what he faced in the moment—rejection by those closest to him, loss of everything familiar, shattered dreams, and an uncertain future. His brothers' vicious betrayal had not been deserved. Maybe he had bragged a little and tattled on his brothers. But surely those things were not sufficient to earn him this cruel mistreatment!

But having no say in the matter, Joseph went along. What else could he do?

When his caravan reached Egypt, Joseph was taken to be auctioned off like an ox. Who would purchase him? How would he be treated? What would his assignment be? And the most haunting question of all: how could the God of his fathers be writing a story for him with even a glimmer of good? His circumstances seemed anything but.

Fear, discouragement, and despair must have all but overwhelmed the young man as he stood on the block. And the years that followed would provide him with back-to-back opportunities for more of the same.

Joseph was led away, purchased by a senior official named Potiphar, the "captain of the guard"—most likely in charge of those who protected the Pharaoh. He also may have managed the prison for those who, for one reason or another, had displeased the Egyptian despot and been incarcerated.[1]

From our vantage point over three millennia later, we can see the purposes of God carefully being brought to pass in and through Joseph's life. But for him at the time, there must have been little more than unanswered questions, unjust circumstances over which he had no control, continuing year after year.

Yet we know something important about Joseph's situation—something he could only have grasped by faith. We know that "the LORD was with Joseph" (Gen. 39:2). That reality made all the difference in the world and in the outcome of Joseph's story.

As we reflect on that story, we see God's unmistakable hand. His sovereign pen. For you see, this story is not simply about one man. As with each story God writes, Joseph's story is part of the unfolding of a grander plot involving Joseph's brothers, his father, the rescue of a family from starvation, a lesson in forgiveness and reconciliation, and also, eventually, the salvation of a nation from four hundred years of slavery and abuse.

More times than I (Nancy) can count, I have shared with others something unforgettable I heard pastor John Piper say many years ago:

In every situation you face, God is always doing a thousand different things that you cannot see and you do not know.

Oh, if we think hard, we may be able to discern a *few* things He is doing in the midst of the mess around us. Looking back—that rearview mirror again—we might be able to see a few more. But unseen and unknown to us, He is in fact doing *a thousand* or more things. Things that will one day become clear to us, either in this world or the next. Things that will cause us to exclaim in worship, "You have done all things well!" (see Mark 7:37).

> Doubtless, had he been given the opportunity, Joseph would have written a different plot. But with each twist and turn of his story, this young man was being shaped and transformed by God.

Perhaps from where you sit today, you can see only miscellaneous, frayed, disconnected strands that make no sense at all, no matter how hard you try to figure it all out. All you can see is injustice and pain. Our young friend Joseph would surely have identified with you.

But as Joseph would one day learn, on the flip side of the tapestry God is weaving in and through our lives—the tangle of threads that we can see—He is creating a picture of great beauty and worth for those who will trust Him.

From the purchase of Joseph on the auction block, we follow him to Potiphar's home. He was actually owned by this influential man, a piece of property with no power to control or change his circumstances. But in spite of having no ability to govern his fate, Joseph did what he was able to do, which was to govern *himself.* When it would have been natural—and understandable—for Joseph to lash out in anger or collapse in a heap of whining despair, he stood firm. He handled his duties with unflagging integrity, and his master soon took notice, giving him more and more freedom and responsibility. Eventually Potiphar even made Joseph overseer of his household.

Finally, life was going well for Joseph—but then trouble struck again.

With full knowledge of God's plan for Joseph, the archenemy of his soul sent a desperate housewife, Potiphar's wife, to lure him into an act of fornication (adultery for her). Joseph managed to hold on to his virtue and refused to submit to sin. But what was his reward for obeying God's law and respecting his master? A false accusation and then thirteen years in prison!

Doubtless, had he been given the opportunity, Joseph would have written a different plot. But with each twist and turn of his story, this young man was being shaped and transformed by God. Psalm 105 describes this remarkable progression:

> [The Lord] had sent a man ahead of them—
> Joseph, who was sold as a slave.
> They hurt his feet with shackles;
> his neck was put in an iron collar.
> Until the time his prediction came true,
> the word of the LORD tested him. (vv. 17–19 CSB)

The beloved of his father, the young man who dreamed he would one day be exalted as the ruler of his nation, was "sent ahead" by God to a foreign land where, unknown to anyone including Joseph himself, God intended to use him to provide for His people. Once there, in what seemed like a failure of God's plan, Joseph was sold and shackled as a slave. And there, in those horrendous circumstances, the "word of the Lord tested him"—shaped him, honed him—until the time (*God's* time) came for God's predictions through him to be fulfilled.

Taking this message to heart can make a huge difference as you navigate your own challenges and disappointments. The hardest parts of the story God is writing in your life are not random or meaningless. They are full of purpose. And in due time, all that He has intended for you and for this world will come true. In the meantime, He will always be with you. That's a truth you can always trust.

While Joseph was in prison, Pharaoh had two dreams for which no interpretation could be found. Not even the wisest men of the land could discern their meaning. This hopeless search, along with the dreams themselves, troubled the monarch deeply.

Finally a man who had known Joseph in prison—the Pharaoh's cupbearer—recalled his fellow inmate's ability to understand the unknown. Joseph was summoned from prison.

Now Joseph stood before the most powerful man on the face of the earth—a lowly Jew with no standing or rank, in the presence of unvarnished power. This could have been a moment for Joseph to put in a good word for himself, a chance for some long-denied self-promotion. But Joseph chose another way.

> And Pharaoh said to Joseph, "I have . . . heard it said of you that when you hear a dream you can interpret it." Joseph answered Pharaoh, "It is not in me; God will give Pharaoh a favorable answer." (Gen. 41:15–16)

When faced with a perfect opportunity to exalt himself after years of being pushed down, Joseph instead lifted his eyes toward heaven. He trusted the Author of his story.

From there, God's plan for Joseph began revealing itself more clearly. Having revealed the meaning of Pharaoh's dream (with God's help), Joseph was put in charge of preparing Egypt for the famine the dreams had predicted.

Trusting God had rescued him from slavery and prison and put him in a position of power. It also put him in a place where he could have chosen to seek revenge from the brothers who had mistreated him. But instead, Joseph chose to embrace God's hand of Providence. He had developed a perspective that enabled him to rise above the evil that had been done to him.

> The hardest parts of the story God is writing in your life are not random or meaningless. They are full of purpose. ... And in due time, all that He has intended for you and for this world will come true. In the meantime, He will always be with you. That's a truth you can always trust.

Joseph said to his brothers, "Come near to me, please. . . .
I am your brother, Joseph,
whom you sold into Egypt.
And now do not be distressed or angry with yourselves
because you sold me here,
for God sent me before you
to preserve life." (Gen. 45:4–5)

You *sold* me. But God *sent* me.

Joseph later expressed the same perspective when he refused to retaliate against those who had once sought to destroy him:

Joseph said to them. . . . "You meant evil against me, but God meant it for good, to bring it about that many people should be kept alive." (Gen. 50:19–20)

Eventually, long after Joseph's death, it became clear that the story God had written in the life of this patriarch foreshadowed another, far greater Story.

The beloved, favored Son of the Father of life was also envied and mistreated by His brothers. Though He had done no evil and had steadfastly refused the tempter's lure, He was sold for a pittance, cruelly abused, and violently murdered.

We sold Him. But God sent Him.

We meant evil against Him—but God meant it for good, to bring about life for many who were destined to die, that they might become His sons as well.

What a wonder this Story is!

CHAPTER 11

You Can Trust God When Your Child Breaks Your Heart

*If, in dealing with your children's problems,
you find your stomach knotting,
your head pounding, and your teeth clenched,
discover the simple remedy of bending your knees.*

ROBERT J. MORGAN

Losing a child to death is every parent's greatest fear. But as countless distressed parents will testify, there is more than one way to lose a child.

One of the best-known parables Jesus told was the one about a father losing a son. We know it as the story of the prodigal son, but it could also be called the story of the brokenhearted, waiting father.

In the fifteenth chapter of the gospel of Luke, Jesus tells three stories about lost things. There's one about a coin misplaced in a house and a woman who vigorously swept the floor until it was found. It's easy to sum that story up: lost coin, found coin.

Then there's one about a sheep that wandered off, maybe innocently looking for a better patch of grass to nibble on. From there it spotted another patch just a little way off, then another.

Soon the critter was unable to find its way home, and the shepherd was compelled to go searching. Lost sheep, found sheep.

But the lost thing in the third story was far more precious than copper currency or a curious lamb could ever be. Unlike the coin or the sheep, the son in the story made a conscious decision to break his father's heart—and though we don't read anything about her, undoubtedly his mother's as well.

Unlike the woman who lost a coin or the shepherd who lost a sheep, as far as we know the father of the lost boy didn't go on a desperate search for his lost treasure. He didn't gather a posse to bring his son home. Instead, he did the one thing that can be the hardest thing to do in such a situation. He waited. The heartbroken dad in Jesus' parable patiently waited for God to write his own story as well as that of his hardhearted, rebellious, but nonetheless dearly loved offspring.

Every night, before we fall asleep, we hold each other and have a short time of prayer together. (Being a super-early riser, Robert is typically down for the count as soon as the final amen is said.) We thank the Lord for the blessings of our day and lay before Him any major concerns that may have surfaced. We pray for each member of our family, and finally Robert lifts up the names of sixteen young men that He has placed on our hearts. Most of them are adult children of friends of ours. Some of these have never known the Lord. Some have walked away from a faith they once professed. Some (not all) are prodigals, living in "the far country."

In preparing to write this chapter, we talked with two couples whose sons we pray for each night. We asked these parents how they are trusting God with their adult children who have made sinful choices and are currently estranged from their family—situations in which there appears to be no end in sight.

◦⌒◦

"*Scot and Katrina*" have three grown sons, two of whom are married. They have five grandkids thus far—and they'll show you some really cute photos on their phones anytime you're interested. I (Nancy) have known this family since the boys were little and have watched them grow up.

Scot is a master carpenter, and Katrina is a homemaker and watercolor artist. They both love Christ, are active in ministering to others, and have always been eager for their children to follow and serve the Lord.

> "God has given this experience to us. We have come to receive it as a gift from Him, intended to draw us closer to Him . . . and to give us a ministry to others." (Katrina)

Five years ago, their then-twenty-year-old middle son, "*Derrick*," wrote a letter to Scot and Katrina announcing to them that he was gay. He shared that over the years he had had some close women friends but had never felt any romantic attraction toward them, as he did toward men. He'd struggled against those desires, believing homosexuality to be contrary to Scripture.

Now, however, Derrick had discovered and embraced a book written by a "Christian gay activist" who insisted that the Bible's prohibition against homosexuality was actually talking about uncommitted, promiscuous same-sex relationships. A person could be gay and Christian if he lived in a monogamous relationship, and Derrick was making plans to marry his partner.

The day they received the letter from their son, Scot and Katrina texted and asked if they could meet with me (Nancy) and a couple of other close friends. That evening they shared what was happening. The small band of friends wept and prayed with this devastated couple, wanting to help lift the burden they were bearing as their story was being rewritten.

From the outset, Scot made every attempt to reach out to his son. Knowing Derrick's professed love for Christ, he tried to point out the disconnect between biblical teaching and homosexual relationships. But Derrick, who was quite familiar with the Bible himself, just tossed Bible verses back at his dad. The conversations went nowhere, usually ending abruptly.

The more Scot tried, the clearer it became that Derrick had made up his mind. The contacts became less frequent. Occasionally Katrina would send texts assuring Derrick of her love and prayers for him. Sometimes Derrick texted back. Usually not.

As the four of us sat and talked, Katrina opened her heart about how all this has affected them as a couple:

> This is a chapter of our story that I'd like to rip out, but it's also the chapter God is using most in our lives to help us know His heart . . . and to teach us to love each of our kids and grandkids unconditionally even when we don't understand what is going on.

Scot chimed in thoughtfully:

> We've wrestled with what is our responsibility in this situation. We've asked God to search our hearts. And we have asked Derrick's forgiveness for everything we could think of, for any ways we might have wronged him.

Then he added, "But we have had to accept that we are not responsible for the choices of our adult children."

We asked Scot and Katrina how they would encourage others with adult children who are living in a way they believe to be contrary to God's Word. They shared three freeing conclusions they have come to in their relationship with their son:

1. *"We can't change his heart.* Every person has a switch in his or her heart that only God can flip. Until that happens, nothing will change. We can't make it happen."

2. *"It's not our responsibility to fix our son.* Parents are fixers. For the first two years after our son sent us the letter, we felt we had to find a way to fix the situation—read this book, that post, this article. And we felt that if we couldn't fix it, we were failures. We finally had to make peace with the truth that Derrick was responsible before God for his own choices. If God allows something difficult in our lives, it doesn't require our fixing; it requires our faith."

3. *"We can't quit.* We will continue to love our son. So much is at stake. Many are watching us walk through this—our children and grandchildren, friends who know us well, and others who barely know us at all. We want them to see that Christ sustains us in the hardest of times and that by His grace we can love unconditionally, even as we have been loved by Him."

And how has this experience changed them?

Scot now realizes that many of the people around him are hurting in ways he didn't realize before—people with incredible burdens. His sensitivity toward people he encounters has grown.

Katrina admits that at times in their journey she has questioned God. After the initial shock of their son's announcement, numbness set in. "I didn't even want to pray or read my Bible. But finally the Father's love broke through to my heart." He reminded her of how He has dealt mercifully with her sins and of how great her own need is for a Savior. Little by little the Lord began to soften her heart—toward Him and toward her son.

She has found peace through embracing the fact that God is good and He is sovereign, even in this situation. She and Scot surrendered Derrick to the Lord before he was born. They trusted Him then, and they continue to trust Him now.

"God has given this experience to us," she said. "We have come to receive it as a gift from Him, intended to draw us closer to Him . . . and to give us a ministry to others."

"Yes," Scot added. "At first, we tried to hide our hurt. Not anymore. We have been given so many opportunities to share with hurting people how the Lord has encouraged us and what He has taught us out of our own experience."

"James and Vicki" and I (Nancy) go back a long way and have remained close friends through multiple moves and life changes. James is a successful insurance broker, Vicki an educator whose most significant teaching accomplishment was homeschooling their four children . . . now grown and with their own families. They have regular, healthy contact with all their kids.

All that is, except *"Wesley."* Wesley is far away from home, both geographically and relationally. He is a drug addict, living who knows where.

This situation was not one James and Vicki ever anticipated. Their faith has always been a vital part of their family life—not just on Sunday, but every day of the week. Those who knew them would have agreed that theirs was a loving, engaged home environment, with lots of opportunities and encouragement for their children to develop their interests and skills, good friendships, and a heart for the Lord.

When Wesley turned eighteen, however, James and Vicki noticed a "gradual darkening of his spirit." Their once happy, fun-loving boy seemed preoccupied—morose and distant. He began pulling away from his parents and his younger sister, with whom he had been extremely close.

Then one night around two in the morning, James and Vicki both woke suddenly from a deep sleep. Sensing something was wrong, James looked outside and saw that his son's car was gone. Thinking it might have been stolen, he quickly checked Wesley's bedroom, only to discover his son was not there.

James and Vicki spent the next two hours sitting in the darkness of their living room. They worried about their son. They wept together and prayed for his safety. Finally, close to dawn Wesley returned, surprised to see his parents awake and waiting. Obviously high, he explained that he had met a supplier online and had driven a hundred miles to make a drug deal.

Over the next few days, Wesley told his parents of his introduction to experimental drugs at a party several years before. Since then, using had become a regular and clearly risky lifestyle. His whole world had changed as he became wrapped up with a friend group that supported and shared that lifestyle with him.

The whole time, his parents had been clueless. "How could we not have known this was going on?" they wondered.

> James and Vicki realize that God is writing the story, and in the end, it's not their story that's important. This is going to be His story.

James and Vicki spent many long, restless nights and many challenging days wrestling with hard questions: *What did we do wrong? How could we have done something different? What do we do now?* But nothing they said or did seemed to change the situation. Much as they tried to assure their son of their love and their desire to get help for him, he seemed deaf to their appeals. Before long Wesley moved out of the house to go live with his drug-abusing friends. There was nothing they could do to stop him.

Wesley is now in his late twenties, and James and Vicki haven't seen him for a year or so. They don't even know exactly where he is living. They continue to look for ways to open the door to a relationship, but their son is withdrawn and isolated, and any communication at this point feels superficial. The occasional phone calls have been short and strained. They've received a handful of notes or cards from their son, among them a Father's Day card. These letters are stacked on a bookshelf in their bedroom next to a picture of their lost son. "We see these letters and they remind us to pray," Vicki told us.

While James and Vicki grieve over their son's broken relationship with the Lord and with his family, their hearts have remained tender toward him. That first night when he came home from the drug dealer, James told him, "Wesley, there's nothing you will ever do to keep us from loving you. You're our son, and we will love you forever."

These hurting parents know that though God loaned Wesley to them to raise, he doesn't belong to them—he belongs to God. That helps them walk in hope rather than despair. "He's in God's hands. He can't be anywhere or do anything that God is not fully aware of," James told us. He and Vicki believe God is going to use all of it for His glory.

In the meantime, Wesley's rebellion has been used of God to

do a deep work in his parents' hearts. Vicki shared with us that He has revealed pride in her heart as a parent. "I used to say, 'Our kids aren't going to do this or that.' Now here we are . . . humbled, but also grateful."

They realize that God is writing the story, and in the end, it's not their story that's important. This is going to be His story.

"God doesn't waste anything," James reminded us. "We can rest that God is going to use this . . . in Wesley, in our other kids, and in us. He has allowed us to pillow our heads at night and not be in great distress. God is writing this chapter."

Their prayer is that, like the prodigal son, Wesley will some-day hear God's voice and come to his senses. "We selfishly hope it will be in our lifetime. But it may not be. And most days we're at peace with that."

> These hurting parents know that though God loaned Wesley to them to raise, he doesn't belong to them—he belongs to God. That helps them walk in hope rather than despair.

The situations faced by the two couples we talked with for this chapter have hijacked their lives in a sense. This is not just a matter of dealing with two-year-old temper tantrums or teenage antics. These grown kids are making life-altering choices that deeply impact their parents and siblings. And we could have shared numerous other such stories. Every time I (Nancy) address the issue of prodigal children through my ministry, I receive an avalanche of responses from moms whose hearts are heavy, longing for a son or daughter to return home—to the Lord and to their family.

We also have many friends whose kids are experiencing intense struggles and attacks not necessarily related to sinful or foolish choices on their part. There is no doubt that the enemy wants to have our children and their children. Just recently we joined several other parents on a Zoom call to pray for the adult child of one of the couples who is battling a form of mental illness that could be life-threatening. We cried out to the Lord for this precious young woman and her husband and children. And we prayed for her parents, that God would protect them from fear and discouragement, that they would feel deeply how much He loves their daughter, and that they would cling to Christ and trust the work He is doing in her life, even when they cannot yet see a positive outcome.

> So what can you do? You can let God change you, even as you are longing for Him to change your child. You can pray. You can trust that God is not only writing your story; He is also writing your child's story. You can wait patiently for the Lord to act in His time and His way.

On another recent occasion, several women and I (Nancy) gathered around a mom who is fighting for the soul of her teenage daughter. Once soft and responsive to the Lord, this child is now hardened, resistant, and seemingly unreachable. Together, with tears, we lifted this woman and her daughter up to the Father, praying for mercy and for tailor-made grace to help them in this critical time of need (see Heb. 4:16). The relief on that mother's face as we finished praying was unmistakable. She lifted her hands into the air and exclaimed, "My burden has been lifted!" The battle for her child is not over, but she is being strengthened by reinforcements the Lord sent her way to encourage her to trust in the faithfulness of God even while her daughter is floundering.

Your heart, too, may be breaking over a son or daughter or a grandchild who is being held captive by Satan's lies. You cannot open his eyes; you cannot turn her heart; you cannot make him or her believe that God's ways are good and right and true and that Christ is the all-surpassing treasure, far more valuable than anything the world holds out as desirable.

If that is your struggle, remember what Scot and Katrina came to realize:

- *You cannot change your child's heart.*

- *It's not your responsibility to fix your child.*

- *You can't quit.*

So what *can* you do?

You can let God change you, even as you are longing for Him to change your child.

You can pray.

You can gather a few trusted confidants to join you in pleading with God to break through in your child's life.

You can trust that God is not only writing your story; He is also writing your child's story. And because of this, you can resist the temptation to pick up the pen and take over. Specifically, you can resolve not to interfere in the way the Lord may be dealing with your son or daughter to bring him or her to repentance or to refine faith through hardship.

You can wait patiently for the Lord to act in His time and His way. And you can demonstrate and declare (and remind yourself in the process!) that God is worthy of your worship and trust and that He is still good—even if your heart is breaking, even if your child's heart or circumstances never change in your lifetime.

This is the walk of faith that cherishes and honors the Lord above all other loves.

And this is a powerful legacy you leave to those who are coming behind you.

How have you found God to be faithful
in unexpected or difficult chapters of your life?
Share your story *on your favorite social media platform.*
#TrustGodToWriteYourStory

CHAPTER 12

You Can Trust God When You Lose a Loved One

You either say, "Okay God, I'm on the ride with You"...
or you go off the rails. Because how do you exist
unless you say, "I believe that His Word is true
and that He intends good for me"?

P E G   C A M P B E L L

*W*hite puffy clouds graced the azure sky, the temperature hovered in the high seventies . . . a perfect November day in central Florida. But the setting that had brought close friends and family together at Dr. Phillips Cemetery was anything but idyllic. This moment was something I (Robert) never could have imagined for myself. It's one thing to attend a burial service for an acquaintance. It's another to be seated on the front row, burying your mate.

I sat between my two daughters, holding their hands. The pastor read from a small leather notebook and then closed with a prayer of consecration. Someone in the extended family standing behind us started singing. Voices were raised in sweet harmony:

... There is no shadow of turning with Thee;
Thou changest not, Thy compassions, they fail not;
As Thou has been, Thou forever wilt be.[1]

Bobbie had been my wife for almost forty-five years. We had raised our children together, written books together, supported each other, and fought together through her long illness. Now I was saying goodbye to her for the last time. As the earth slowly swallowed her casket, a strange numbness covered me. Tears flowed freely from my daughters' eyes. Too weary to cry, I stared at the descending box until it rested firmly at the bottom of the freshly dug hole.

I would now add a new title to my name: widower.

This moment was holy, and it was hard. Precious and painful.

Though my family and I were determined to trust God to write the story of our lives, this was not the script we would have composed.

> I would now add a new title to my name: widower. This moment was holy, and it was hard. Precious and painful. (Robert)

How can I move forward when my grief is so overwhelming? The loss of my loved one is so very painful and has left me almost paralyzed.

How I (Nancy) wished I could reach out and hold the woman who sent me this note recently. Her words undoubtedly express what some who are reading this book are experiencing. Perhaps a sense of deep loss prompted you to turn to this chapter first. Though I cannot know or feel exactly what you are going through, death and grief are familiar territory to me. In fact, for a while when I was in my twenties and thirties, it seemed that my family gathered more often for funerals than for any other occasion.

Losing my dad on the weekend of my twenty-first birthday was an enormous loss. He was fifty-three years old, and he left behind a forty-year-old widow and seven children ages eight to twenty-one. Six years later, my mother's mother—the only grandparent I had ever known—died shortly after moving into our home. Less than a year later, we buried my mother's only sibling, who died of a rare lung disease at the age of thirty-eight, leaving a grieving husband and three young children. And then, just over three months later, I received a call with the news that my twenty-two-year-old brother, David, then a junior at Liberty University, had been in a serious automobile accident and was not expected to live.

I immediately flew to Philadelphia, where my handsome, generous, fun-loving "little" brother lay in the ICU in the University of Pennsylvania Hospital on life support. For the next seven days, our family huddled together in that hospital, hoping against hope, hardly knowing how to pray, until David's heart finally stopped beating and we were left with his soulless body.

*

Death is real . . . as is the grief that is always its companion.

Over the years both of us have waited and wept by the side of friends as they released a loved one—an elderly saint at the end of a race well run, a healthy young woman or man struck down in the prime of life, or a days-old infant whose life on earth had barely begun. Perhaps no grief surpasses that of a parent losing a child. Everything within cries out, *It's not supposed to be this way.* But regardless of how expected or unexpected or what the specifics may be, the loss of a loved one is always painful.

I (Nancy) was enjoying a vacation with friends in the Pacific Northwest in September of 1998 when we received word that Anthony Jones had gone missing. His parents, **Tom and Danna Jones,** had been dear friends of mine since Anthony was twelve. (During his teens, this strapping young man liked to tell people he was my personal bodyguard!)

Over the next seventeen days, we all prayed and hoped like crazy for any shred of news as to Anthony's whereabouts.

When Robert and I talked with Tom and Danna about that awful time some twenty years later, the details were still vivid in their minds.

Anthony's disappearance came on the tail end of a long period of stressful and traumatic events. Tom had lost his dad. Danna had suffered major health issues. They had adopted two severely abused children, who adored their big brother, Anthony. But Anthony had also struggled since high school with alcohol addiction.

Recently, though, life had seemed to settle down a little. In God's mercy, Anthony had gone to a Christian treatment home, where he had come to faith in Christ. He had been back home and sober for a year. And though he lived in his own apartment a few miles away, he checked in with his parents every day . . . until one day he didn't.

Another day went by without word from Anthony, then another. Their calls to him went unanswered. He didn't answer his door, and his apartment seemed empty. They were concerned. And afraid.

Soon the police were involved. Local media picked up the story, and many people combed the area, looking for Anthony. There was no sign of him.

Two excruciating weeks passed. Finally, worn out emotionally,

Tom and Danna fell on their knees and begged the Lord to show them where their son was.

The next morning, a Saturday in October, Tom finally went to Anthony's apartment to gather his belongings. Home alone, Danna looked out the front window to see two couples who were close friends, including their pastor and his wife, walking toward the front door.

Danna knew why they had come.

They rang the doorbell, and Danna met them at the door. Her pastor told her that a vehicle matching the description of Anthony's car had been pulled out of a nearby creek. He read off a license plate number.

> Perhaps no grief surpasses that of a parent losing a child. Everything within cries out, *It's not supposed to be this way.*

"Yes, that's Anthony's," Danna said.

The pastor looked tenderly toward Danna. "A body was found in the car."

Danna knew in her heart that it was her son's body. A flood of emotions followed. Of course, she was thankful that he had been found. But at the same time, the loss of hope caused her to groan deeply. "It was so final," she told us.

When Tom returned from Anthony's apartment and saw the somber gathering, he knew too.

"You go into shock," Tom told us. "It's like God's gift to our system, to protect us physically and emotionally. Losing a child is an unnatural order. It messes you up. It seems upside down. Backward."

"At this point," Tom said, "you can either be done with God entirely or be at such a point of need that you totally yield and reach out to Him in a new way." Many choose the former. He and Danna chose the latter.

"From the beginning of our journey," Danna said, "I purposed not to lose my joy, no matter the struggles, heartache, and pain. We wanted to faithfully represent Christ."

But even with that conviction, Tom and Danna's emotions were on a roller coaster. Not long after Anthony was gone, Tom woke up early one morning as the reality that he would never see his boy again hit him afresh. Tom wept uncontrollably. All he could say was, "My son, my son, my son!"

For Danna, it all hit her one day as she sat in Tom's arms on the family-room couch crying out, "My baby, my baby, my baby!"

We know that the death of a child can put a huge strain on a marriage—sometimes to the breaking point. But Anthony's death bound these two together more closely. As they clung to the Lord, they clung to each other as well. And again and again, they saw Him orchestrate ways to make Himself known to them—and through them to others.

Three years into their loss, Danna came to what she called a "pivotal point." Looking out her kitchen window one day, she said to the Lord: "Why did You take my son? I want my son! Your Son died, but You knew Your Son was going to rise again."

Then she sensed the Father's still small voice in her heart: *I gave you My Son, and your son will also rise again.*

This moment settled in Danna's heart a confidence that God was doing a good thing and that she and Tom would see their son again.

"Losing a child qualifies you to join a club you don't want to be a part of," Danna told us as we talked with her and Tom about their whole experience. "The membership fee is far too high. And it's a lonely place to be, especially when you get together with your friends, listening to all the things their children are doing, thinking of the life you'd hoped to have with your child."

But Danna and Tom have never lost the conviction that God had a purpose for taking them through this process, and they remain committed to trusting Him to write all of their story, even the most painful parts. "Life isn't like a buffet," Tom reflected, "where you get to slide your tray down the polished chrome rails and pick out what you want." He spoke for both of them when he said:

> The sovereignty of God is the foundation of everything for me now. That is what sustains. He writes the story. He is the Author and the Finisher of our faith. It's literally true.

The loss of a child is always devastating, no matter how old or young the child may be.

Chase and Katie Kemp's son, Job (like the Bible name), was five years old when he was diagnosed with a large, aggressive brain tumor. Over the next 135 days, this child captured the heart of his entire church family as he waged a valiant battle with this ferocious form of childhood cancer. He passed away shortly before his sixth birthday.

A close friend of ours, Jennifer, who had been Job's preschool Sunday school teacher and walked through this loss with this family, shared with us an unforgettable moment in the memorial service for this dearly loved child. At one point in the service, Chase rose from his seat on the front row. He is a tall man, and Jennifer immediately thought of something little Job had said to her a year or so earlier.

One Sunday morning Job had shown up for class sporting new shoes—shoes that looked less like little-kid shoes and more like a small version of men's boots. He'd proudly showed them to "Miss Jennifer" and told her that one day his feet were going to be as big as his daddy's.

That memory came to Jennifer's mind as Chase walked to the microphone to recite Scripture in honor of his son, who everyone now knew would not grow to be as big as his daddy.

"I was angry," Jennifer remembered. "I was weeping—full of grief and confusion."

And then these words came forth from this grieving dad's mouth—each word intensely spoken and filled with deep emotion:

> Bless the LORD, O my soul,
>   and all that is within me,
>   bless his holy name!

With a booming voice and his arms open wide, Chase went on to recite all twenty-two verses of Psalm 103. At many points, he beat his chest with his big, strong arms as he fought through his grief to affirm what he knew to be true.

In his palpable pain, Chase led his young family and the whole congregation in worshiping the Lord. Those in attendance that day—like Jennifer—will never forget that powerful message.

Little Job had looked so much like his daddy, so looking at Chase had almost been like seeing Job's future. Now it was clear that future would never be. It didn't make sense then, and it doesn't make sense now to Job's mom and dad and siblings or to their extended church family.

And yet, Jennifer told us,

> In the midst of our grief, we bless the Lord. We trust the Lord. We remember how God gave this special boy an extraordinary ability to perceive His nature and character even as a three-year-old, when he was asking questions about the Trinity and wanting me to draw it for him. We know Job knew God. And we know that Job is with God today.

Job's death came so much sooner than anyone could have anticipated. He never got to have feet as big as his daddy's. Yet the impact of his short life and of his death was profound:

> As a father shows compassion to his children,
>   So the LORD shows compassion to those who fear him.
>   (Ps. 103:13)

On February 14, 2005, I (Nancy) sat in a hospital waiting room in Anaheim, California, alongside friends and family members of Jon Campbell, who was undergoing radical surgery to remove his esophagus.

Just down the road, at the Anaheim Convention Center, thousands of attendees at the National Religious Broadcasters annual convention were praying earnestly for this beloved colleague and friend, who was battling for his life.

Along with his wife, Peg, and her brother, Jim, Jon led Ambassador Advertising Agency, an organization that serves many Christian broadcasters and the ministries they represent. But now he was in a fight for his life. Having survived a rough two-year bout of Hodgkin's disease twenty-five years earlier, he had recently been diagnosed with esophageal cancer. Survival rate for someone in his condition at that point: 4 percent.

In the wake of the diagnosis, **Peg Campbell** recalls a sense of her life spinning out of control while she did her best to provide the support Jon needed in the stiff headwinds they were facing. One of the hardest moments was the day they went together to an outpatient clinic to have a port put in for chemo following Jon's surgery.

"I just can't do the chemo," Jon decided as they sat in the clinic waiting room. He was completely worn out. The prognosis was so grave, and they had both been in the battle for so long. At best the chemo would only delay the inevitable. Peg, of course, wanted Jon to keep fighting, but she also wanted to respect his choice to decline further treatment. They both knew this meant that, barring divine intervention, they would be facing his death sooner than later.

Jon would live another four months after the surgery before the Lord took him home. It was a miserable four months, marked by excruciating pain.

But in the middle of the grim realities at hand, there were also moments of laughter and hours of singing with Peg's mom at the piano and her dad close by. A few days before Jon died, they were joined by their dear friends Ken and Joni Tada along with other family members, as they sang together in the Campbells' living room.

> God has something purposeful in mind for you in this situation. What is it that He intends for you to fulfill that would not be possible if you had not suffered this loss?
> (Peg Campbell)

Peg remembers it as a "sacred gathering," but she also recalls how frail Jon looked as he sat with eyes closed, listening to the singing. "Dying is not a beautiful thing," she told us. "It's very, very, very hard."

If you've been through this with a loved one, you understand. Through most of life, no matter what challenge we face, there's a thread of hopefulness that somehow it will be better—a relationship will be restored, finances will improve. But death severs that thread. "The guillotine drops. One side is truncated from the other."

On June 22, 2005, Jon passed from this life to the next, leaving those who loved him to grapple with the pain of living without him. "I will never hold Jon's hand again," Peg told us quietly.

In an email update written exactly one year after Jon's death, Peg didn't try to sugarcoat her experience:

> In many ways I feel like the full-speed runner who hit a wall and is now reeling, trying to regain footing . . . or the swimmer in a roiling sea, hit by wave after wave—*glub, glub, glub*. What I desperately covet is knowing how to maintain equilibrium in the midst of being completely turned upside down and inside out.

With Jon's passing, Peg's life has indeed changed dramatically. "This is not a new chapter; it's a whole new book," she says. But day by day, as those of us who know and love her can attest, she has managed to press on with remarkable grace, trusting God to write her story beyond the chapter that included Jon.

One of the changes in Peg's life has involved an opportunity to teach and mentor students at a Christian university. She shares with them her story as well as an acrostic she has dubbed her "G.R.A.C.E. Toolkit." The five elements spelled out by this mnemonic device have helped her get a handle on surviving—and thriving in—her new reality:

Gratitude Refuse moaning, anger, and perpetual sadness (however understandable it may seem) and choose instead to have a spirit of gratitude.

Relationships Community is one of the ways in which God infuses grace into our lives and anchors our hearts.

Achievements Trust that He will provide the strength and grace needed to do whatever is required of you.

Calling God has something purposeful in mind for you in

this situation. What is it that He intends for you to fulfill that would not be possible if you had not suffered this loss?

Eternal Perspective Keep an eternal focus and orientation each day of your life here on earth.

Peg doesn't ever want to lose the very real gifts that bereavement has brought her. "The grieving process is sacred territory," Peg reminded us. "It's too easy to return to normality and forget the intimacy with Jesus you experienced in your deepest distress"—something she is determined not to let happen.

George Müller (1805–1898) is remembered for establishing homes to care for thousands of orphans in Bristol, England, and for trusting God to meet the needs of the children as well as the numerous other ministries he founded and oversaw.

Throughout his long life, Müller maintained deep confidence in the goodness and sovereignty of God. But that did not exempt him from intense suffering and trials. He endured seasons of great physical pain. He also outlived two wives whom he dearly loved.

Müller's first wife, Mary, bore him four children, two of whom were stillborn and one of whom died when he was a year old. After thirty-nine years of marriage, Mary died of rheumatic fever. Within a few hours of her death, Müller went to an evening prayer meeting in Salem Chapel, where he offered up prayer and praise to the Lord. Five days later, standing before some twelve hundred orphans and thousands of grieving friends, he preached the sermon at his wife's funeral. His text was Psalm 119:68:

> Thou art good, and doest good. (KJV)

This verse is particularly precious to me (Nancy). On September 1, 1979, when I received the call that my dad had just died of a heart attack, the first conscious thought that crossed my mind—before the enormous sense of loss that would follow—was this verse, which I had read days earlier and which God in His kindness now brought to mind. In that moment, and many times since, this assurance has been an anchor for my aching heart.

Müller's funeral message included three simple points based on that very same verse:

> I. The Lord was good and did good in giving [my wife] to me.
> II. The Lord was good and did good in so long leaving her to me.
> III. The Lord was good and did good in taking her from me.[2]

Reflecting later on this trial, Müller wrote,

> My heart was at rest and my heart was satisfied with God.
> And all this springs . . . from taking God at His Word,
> believing what He says.[3]

In every season and circumstance, including times of deep grief and pain, George Müller trusted the sovereignty and goodness of God. That made all the difference in his life, as it does today in our lives and in yours.

*How have you found God to be faithful
in unexpected or difficult chapters of your life?*
Share your story *on your favorite social media platform.*
#TrustGodToWriteYourStory

CHAPTER 13

You Can Trust God When You're Facing Death

Only when our greatest love is God,
a love that we cannot lose even in death,
can we face all things with peace.

Tim Keller

orn in 1914, Professor Gladys Greathouse was iconic at Taylor University, where she chaired the drama department and oversaw the school's theatrical productions in the 1960s. Until my (Robert's) senior year in high school, I had no interest in this field. But after some platform time at our variety show, the acting bug started nibbling. So when I got to Taylor in 1965, I signed up to perform in a play.

In the weeks leading up to our performance, I learned that this woman with a funny last name was both kind and tough. She loved her students and proved it with tenacious discipline. Barely five feet tall, Gladys was a tower of resolve and strength.

What I remember most about her was her insistence on focused practices. As we met in a dingy downstairs classroom and began reading our lines and blocking our movements, absolutely no horseplay was tolerated.

"If you practice well," she'd say, *"you'll perform well."*

Those words have remained seared in my memory, and I've learned they apply to a lot more than getting ready for a college play.

More than fifty years after receiving that advice from Gladys Greathouse, on a warm Michigan summer afternoon, we visited with two dear friends in their home. Nancy had known **John and Tammy Wreford** since before they were married in the 1980s and had shared many life experiences with these humble, faithful followers of Christ.

> "If you practice well, you'll perform well."
> (Gladys Greathouse)

Tammy met us at the door. We looked into the living room and saw John seated in his recliner. He called out his welcome.

As we approached our friend, we were taken aback by what we saw. John's skin stretched over a swollen frame like transparent white parchment. Wisps of thinning, tousled white hair rested on top of his head, and weeks' worth of scraggly white beard covered his cheeks, chin, and neck. He had been told he had weeks or less to live. Hospice had taken over his care, helping to keep him comfortable in his final days.

For months we had watched this couple go through difficult, deep waters with extraordinary calm and fortitude, and we had asked if they would talk with us about what it looks like to trust God when you're facing death.

Scooching two chairs close to John's, we sat facing him, his almost luminescent white legs elevated directly in front of us. Tammy took her place in a chair next to her husband. Gently laying a hand on John's bare ankle, Robert started our visit by thanking the Lord for John and Tammy and for their steadfast faith throughout the tiresome journey they had been on.

Then the four of us talked.

We reviewed the time line of John's illness, from the time (fourteen months earlier) he first learned about his escalated PSA number and received the prostate-cancer diagnosis. He and Tammy told us of the complex, sometimes frustrating, maze they had navigated since then—doctors, clinics, scans, needles, infusions, and medications with unpronounceable names.

John spoke thoughtfully, his British accent still evident (he grew up in Zimbabwe when it was still British Rhodesia), his countenance focused. Occasionally he took a sip from the water bottle on the table next to him. We waited as he swallowed carefully.

John told us that he had made a profession of faith as a young teen but had not fully surrendered his life to Christ until years later. He also talked about some of his life's challenges, including losing his first wife suddenly to a suspected brain aneurysm just eighteen months after they were married.

After a bit more conversation, Robert asked John, "If you were sitting where I'm sitting and I was where you are, what would you say to me?"

John sat quietly for a few moments before responding.

"I'd tell you," he began, "that dealing with this illness isn't something you start when you are diagnosed. That moment is a continuation of a journey that starts years earlier."

He paused, then went on.

> God has blessed us in so many ways through the years. But we live in a sinful world, so bad things happen. We have to

take the good with the bad, trusting that God knows what He's doing and that He's in control.

He told us that as the cancer progressed and the treatments didn't seem to be working, he had realized he had a choice:

> I could have responded by saying, "Why me?" A lot of people do that. Or I could say, "God, what are You wanting to accomplish through this?" That is the way I've tried to live my life in recent years. So I've been okay with this diagnosis since day one.

Gladys Greathouse couldn't have said it better. "If you practice well, you'll perform well."

"And what about the next few weeks?" we asked. "What about your death?"

"I'm not afraid of death," he said without hesitation. "I'm not anxious." Then, after a deep breath, "But I'm not looking forward to what my final days could be like."

Tammy's eyes welled with tears. Ours did too.

⌀───⌀

John was not alone in those feelings. Days earlier I (Nancy) had asked a group of women to share some of the challenges of getting older. One of the women spoke for many in the room when she said, "I'm not afraid of death, but I'm anxious about dying." And we can certainly relate to some trepidation about how it will all go down. Will there be pain? Will we be alone? Will we be afraid?

No one except God Himself knows the answers to those questions, of course. But we have found comfort and inspiration in John Bunyan's immortal allegory, *The Pilgrim's Progress*, first published in 1678. This classic tale chronicles the journey of a character named Christian as he travels toward the Celestial City.

He endures one harrowing trial and temptation after another on his journey, but finally he and his companion, Hopeful, draw near to their destination. (In allegorical terms, this parallels our approach to death.)

One might assume that this final stretch would be easy, but not so. The sight of the deep, swift river that flows between the pilgrims and the gate to the City causes Christian no small amount of anxiety.

Bunyan's description is exquisite as he describes Christian's trepidation (and ours) over crossing this barrier:

> The pilgrims then, especially Christian, began to despond in their mind, and looked this way and that, but no way could be found by them by which they might escape the River. . . . Then they addressed themselves to the water, and entering, Christian began to sink, and crying out to his good friend Hopeful, he said, "I sink in deep waters; the billows go over my head. . . .
>
> Then said the other, "Be of good cheer, my brother; I feel the bottom, and it is good." . . . Hopeful would also endeavor to comfort him, saying, "Brother, I see the Gate, and men standing by to receive us. . . . These troubles and distresses that you go through in these waters, are no sign that God hath forsaken you; but are sent to try you, whether you will call to mind that which heretofore you have received of his goodness, and live upon him in your distresses." . . .
>
> Then they both took courage, and the enemy was after that as still as a stone, until they were gone over. Christian, therefore, presently found ground to stand upon, and so it followed that the rest of the River was but shallow. Thus they got over.[1]

"Be of good cheer, my brother; I feel the bottom, and it is good." This is the message our friend John consistently shared with those around him, as he was in the process of crossing that river to his eternal home. He was not glib or in denial about death, but he was confident in the presence of Christ with him each step of the way.

Our conversation with John and Tammy in their home ended with a tender prayer. We asked the Father to grant John safe and gentle passage to heaven and to draw near to his fifty-five-year-old wife who, barring divine intervention, would soon be widowed.

> The key to experiencing peace in the final pages of our life on earth is to trust Him in the earlier chapters.

As we left we realized this would likely be the last time we'd see John here on earth. On our way home, we talked about what lay ahead for him in his final days here on earth and then in heaven. And we talked about a moving scene in the 2003 film *The Lord of the Rings: The Return of the King*, the final installment in Peter Jackson's masterful adaptation of J. R. R. Tolkien's Lord of the Rings trilogy.

A hobbit named Pippin and the wizard Gandalf lean into each other, each with his eyes intently locked on the other, as a fierce enemy closes in around them, death pummeling their door. Pippin quietly laments, "I didn't think it would end this way."

"End?" Gandalf probes. "No, the journey doesn't end here. Death is just another path . . . one that we all must take. The grey rain-curtain of this world rolls back, and all turns to silver glass . . . and then you see it."

"What? Gandalf? . . . See what?"

"White shores . . . and beyond, a far green country under a swift sunrise."

"Well, that isn't so bad."

"No . . . no, it isn't." [2]

During our unforgettable visit with John Wreford, we were reminded that we have a strong assurance of what lies beyond "the grey rain-curtain of this world"—maybe not the details, but the essence.

And where do we get that assurance? The key to experiencing peace in the final pages of our life on earth is to trust Him in the earlier chapters. And keeping in view what lies ahead will enable us to trust when the plot we see unfolding is difficult to embrace.

The experience that awaited Bunyan's two pilgrims on the other side of that raging river made their long, hard journey more than worth it. In fact, it was the point of the whole journey.

> Now I saw in my dream, that these two men went in at the Gate; and lo, as they entered, they were transfigured; and they had raiment put on that shone like gold. There were also that met them with harps and crowns, and gave them to them; the harps to praise withal, and the crowns in token of honor.
>
> Then I heard in my dream, that all the bells in the City rang again for joy, and that it was said unto them, "Enter ye into the joy of your Lord" (Matt. 25:23). . . .
>
> Now, just as the Gates were opened to let in the men, I looked in after them, and behold, the City shone like the sun; the streets also were paved with gold; and in them walked many men, with crowns on their heads, palms in their hands, and golden harps, to sing praises withal.
>
> There were also of them that had wings, and they answered one another without intermission, saying, "Holy, holy, holy is the Lord" (Rev. 4:8). And after that they shut up the Gates; which, when I had seen, I wished myself among them.[3]

> None of us can know in advance what God has planned regarding the circumstances and timing of our death. What we do know is that our times are in His hand and that every day of our lives was ordained and planned by Him before the day of our birth.

Exactly three weeks after our visit, our friend John passed over to the other side. Several days later, we waited in line to comfort his widow, his young adult son, and other family members. We hugged Tammy, assured her of our love and prayers, and commented on the way she and John had demonstrated pure, simple trust as the Lord was writing their story. With a sincere smile, she said to us, "I've been singing! It has to be His grace." Amazing grace.

One of the most touching moments in the memorial service the next morning was watching a video clip from an interview a colleague had recorded with John about five months earlier. With a steady voice, John said,

> I want to finish the race well. No matter what happens, God is in control. If it's my time to die, I want to glorify God in dying and show people He's still faithful and He's still good. [4]

In one sense the story God wrote for John is now finished. He has no more pain, no more medical merry-go-round to endure, no more concern about what the future holds. He is at home with the One he trusted to write his story.

But in another sense, of course, John's story is not finished, for he is still very much alive. He will spend eternity worshiping and serving the Christ he worshiped and served here on earth. And God is still at work in the lives of those John left behind—those he loved and prayed for while he was still with us—continuing to exalt His Son through the story He is writing through them.

Rarely have we seen anyone face death with such tranquility and quiet assurance as we witnessed in John (and Tammy) over his last fourteen months. They beautifully and faithfully showed us that for those who are in Christ, death has truly lost its sting.

None of us can know in advance what God has planned regarding the circumstances and timing of our death. What we do know is that our times are in His hand and that every day of our lives was ordained and planned by Him before the day of our birth (see Pss. 31:15 and 139:16). While suffering devastating loss and excruciating pain and while longing at times for death to deliver him from his torment, Job affirmed this:

> A person's days are determined
> and the number of his months depends on you,
> and . . . you have set limits he cannot pass. (Job 14:5 CSB)

The good news of the gospel is that through His death on the cross, our Savior put death to death and ensured that all who trust in Him would live forever. This is the promise He had made to His dear friend Martha, who was grieving the death of her brother, Lazarus:

> I am the resurrection and the life. Whoever believes in me,
> though he die, yet shall he live, and everyone who lives and
> believes in me shall never die. Do you believe this?
> (John 11:25–26)

Do you believe this? Whether we are facing our own death or the death of a loved one who trusted in Christ, that is the question He asks us.

I've never forgotten a statement made by a friend who spoke at my brother's memorial service decades ago: "We tend to think that David has gone from the land of the living to the land of the dead; but the truth is that he has gone from the land of the dying to the land of the living."

Do you believe that?

If you do, the death of a believer takes on a whole different perspective.

The pain of grief and loss is real, but so is the peace of knowing that the Savior who conquered death is holding both you and the one who has gone ahead of you in His loving arms.

*How have you found God to be faithful
in unexpected or difficult chapters of your life?*
Share your story *on your favorite social media platform.*
#TrustGodToWriteYourStory

CHAPTER 14

Surprised

Mary and Joseph's Story

God doesn't call us to be comfortable.
He calls us to trust Him so completely that we are
unafraid to put ourselves in situations where we
will be in trouble if He doesn't come through.

FRANCIS CHAN

After four hundred years of deafening silence, God's people had all but given up any thought of hearing His voice again.

Gone were the days of the Creator speaking with His loved ones in the garden . . . or from atop Mount Sinai in thunder and lightning . . . or in the bush that burned yet was not consumed . . . or through His servants the prophets . . . or in dreams and visions. All these seemed like no more than once-upon-a-time stories.

And now there was nothing, not even a still, small voice. No one alive knew anyone who knew anyone who had ever actually heard Him speak.

So what had become of all God's promises—that the head of the serpent would be crushed? That the desert would be turned into a fruitful place? That every unrighteous oppressor would be judged, His people's sins would be forgiven, their hearts of stone would be turned into hearts of flesh, and they would become a light to the nations?

What about His pledge to send an "anointed one" (Isa. 61:1)? A Messiah who would

> bring good news to the poor . . .
>   to bind up the brokenhearted,
> to proclaim liberty to the captives,
>   and the opening of the prison to those who are bound . . .
>   to comfort all who mourn. (Isa. 61:1–2)

As far as God's people could tell, none of that was even close to happening. Instead, Rome reigned with an iron fist. Sickness and death, oppression and deception left people hopeless and lifeless. And religion, far from providing guidance and comfort, had become institutionalized, impotent, and empty.

Had the God of history forgotten His people entirely?

No, He was getting everything ready for the climax of His story:

> When the fullness of the time had come, God sent forth His Son, born of a woman. (Gal. 4:4 NKJV)

In the tiny, sleepy, Galilean village of Nazareth, a young Jewish woman, perhaps just fourteen years old, was betrothed to a man named Joseph. This was not your modern-day, boy-meets-girl romance. It was more likely the result of two sets of parents meeting for a meal, comparing notes, and determining that their children should marry.

Still, the girl's hopes and dreams would not have been all that different from any other young woman about to be married. What would her life be like? Would she and her husband get along? Would she have children? What did God have in store for her?

We're not told what Mary was doing or exactly where she was at the time of the visitation. The Scripture simply says that "the angel Gabriel was sent from God . . . to a virgin" (Luke 1:26–27).

This is not the first time this celestial being appears in the pages of Scripture. The Old Testament book of Daniel describes another visit:

> And behold, there stood before me [Daniel] one having the appearance of a man. And I heard a man's voice . . . and it called, "Gabriel, make this man understand the vision." So he came near where I stood. And when he came, I was frightened and fell on my face. (Dan. 8:15–17)

Remember this is the same Daniel who spent a peaceful, fearless night cuddled up with a pride of hungry lions. The fact that he was cowed by Gabriel's appearance tells us that this divine courier was no ordinary being.

The next time we meet Gabriel, he's appearing to Zechariah the priest. Like Daniel, Zechariah was "troubled when he saw him, and fear fell upon him" (Luke 1:12). The angel delivered to the priest the news that his wife, Elizabeth, was to conceive their longed-for son. Elizabeth was past childbearing age, so this was a big surprise. Zechariah had a hard time wrapping his head around the message. In fact, he openly doubted God's messenger, who pronounced speechlessness on the priest until the baby was born.

Then we have Gabriel's visit with Mary. Given what we know about this imposing creature, is it any wonder that she would have been afraid? But the angel quickly sought to calm her fear and to assure her that God had an extraordinary mission for her life:

> Do not be afraid, Mary, for you have found favor with God.
> And behold, you will conceive in your womb and bear a son,
> and you shall call his name Jesus. He will be great and will be
> called the Son of the Most High. (Luke 1:30–32)

What a remarkable message. But just as remarkable was Mary's response. For in that moment this young girl relinquished her hold on the script she had assumed would be hers, allowing God to write His Story on the tablet of her life. Mary's response to this astonishing news was simple, humble, and trusting: "Behold, I am the servant of the Lord; let it be to me according to your word" (Luke 1:38).

"Yes, Lord."

What other response is appropriate when the God of the universe speaks? When He says, "I want to use you to be a part of my redemptive plan on earth" . . . when He asks us to lay down our plans and dreams for the sake of His kingdom . . . when He assigns us a task that is far beyond our human capacity. . . .

Yes, Lord.

✦

Joseph, a simple carpenter, had just been stunned with the news that his fiancée, Mary, was pregnant. Scripture doesn't disclose how Joseph was informed of this embarrassing development, but stories and gossip would have traveled quickly in a small town like Nazareth.

With this information that turned his world upside down, there were two things this "just man"[1] (Matt. 1:19) knew for sure: (1) he was not the father of the baby now growing inside Mary, and (2) the law was clear. By Jewish law, Mary could even be executed if charged with fornication.

One can only imagine how crushed Joseph must have been,

believing that his betrothed wife had been with another man and that she might well be lost to him forever. It's surprising that Joseph was sleeping at all.

We don't know how long it was before Gabriel appeared to Joseph in a dream, but it would not have been surprising for a merciful God to move quickly to send comfort and clarity to this humble man.

Because dreams seem so real, so much bigger than life, we can assume that the appearance of this mighty messenger from heaven would have been petrifying to Joseph. But in the end, the message from the angel must have deeply comforted him.

> Mary recognized that she was living in one minuscule moment in a vast eternal scheme of things, orchestrated and ordered by God Himself.

"Do not fear." The angel's first words to Joseph in Matthew 1:20 (the same words he had spoken earlier to Mary) were intended to encourage Jesus' earthly father to trust the outcome of the story his Father was writing. And isn't that always the message of God to our hearts when we are faced with unexpected twists and turns in our own stories? *Don't be afraid!*

Joseph's response to the angel's message reveals his heart: "When [he] woke from sleep, he did as the angel of the Lord commanded him: he took his wife" (Matt. 1:24). Though he could not fathom how the plotline would unfold or how the obvious obstacles would be overcome, he took God at His word and did as he was told.

The narrative God wrote for Mary and Joseph was anything but easy for them to embrace. As with any husband-in-waiting,

Joseph wanted to be his bride's "first." He wanted to have children with her and raise a family like ordinary folk do. He didn't want there to be any question about his wife's purity. But God's Story challenged all those desires—at least as far as outward appearances went. It took a lot for Joseph to take Mary as his wife when everyone else probably assumed she had slept with someone else.

And like every bride-to-be, Mary had surely dreamed of beginning life as Joseph's wife. She pictured their children playing with their friends on the quiet streets of Nazareth. Now a shroud of shame shadowed her. God's Story changed her plans too.

Yet when God visited these two to announce a change in (their) plans, their response was the same: *Yes, Lord. Though Your script for our lives is totally different from the one we would have written, though we cannot see how You're going to do this, and though we certainly don't know how to explain it to anyone else . . . we trust You.*

<hr />

Shortly after the angelic visitation, Mary traveled south to a town in Judah, to visit her older cousin Elizabeth, Zechariah's wife, whose world had also been rocked by the announcement of an unexpected (impossible!) pregnancy. The two women found in each other the gift of someone who understood what it was to trust God in the midst of the unexplainable.

When the women met, Mary was so overwhelmed and excited by all that was happening that she burst forth in a poem of praise. We know it today as the Magnificat, named after the Latin word found in the first line in her song:

> My soul magnifies the Lord,
>   and my spirit rejoices in God my Savior. (Luke 1:46–47)

Mary's hymn includes no fewer than a dozen quotations and allusions from the Old Testament—particularly remarkable considering that there were no personal copies of the scriptures to read and that Mary likely did not know how to read, anyway. Perhaps she had heard a scribe read them or heard her father quote them. But however she'd learned those scriptures, the point is that in the face of the utterly unanticipated upheaval in her own plans, Mary *worshiped*. She exalted the character of God. She rehearsed and clung to God's promises. She understood that this turn of events was not about her; it was about *Him* and His plan of salvation.

> His mercy is for those who fear him
> from generation to generation. (v. 50)

Mary recognized that she was living in one minuscule moment in a vast eternal scheme of things, orchestrated and ordered by God Himself. His covenant promises were a strand that connected her and Joseph's otherwise insignificant lives to past and future generations. Looking back, she was connected to those who had been the recipients of those promises and had believed God when they could not see the outcome of their faith. Looking forward, she would be a link to the fulfillment of God's promises through the Son she was carrying and to those who would believe in Him for generations yet to come.

> He has helped his servant Israel,
> in remembrance of his mercy,
> as he spoke to our fathers,
> to Abraham and to his offspring forever. (vv. 54–55)

After the initial shock, Mary and Joseph's story continued to be unlike anything they ever would have written for themselves. Right smack in the middle of Mary's pregnancy, for example, the

Roman emperor decreed that everyone must return to their original hometown to participate in a census.

What! How could the timing possibly be worse for an eighty-mile trek from Nazareth to Bethlehem? This makes no sense at all!

No sense at all to their finite understanding. But complete sense to the One who works all things "according to the purpose of his will, to the praise of his glorious grace" (Eph. 1:5–6) . . . the One who had revealed some seven hundred years earlier that the Messiah would be born in Bethlehem (Mic. 5:2).

In the fullness of time . . .

Had the young couple been able to see into the future, they would have realized that their story—with its hardships and mysteries for which there was no human explanation—was far from over.

When they took the eight-day-old infant Jesus to the temple for the ritually required dedication and naming, the elderly Simeon spoke to Mary of trials she was yet to face.

> Mary and Joseph had no idea—nor do we—what the future would hold, but their confidence in the One who held the future was unassailable. So they said *Yes*. And in their obedience, they stepped into pivotal roles in the greater Story God was writing.

> Behold, this child is appointed for the fall and rising of many in Israel, and for a sign that is opposed (and a sword will pierce through your own soul also). (Luke 2:34–35)

As the teen mom received her newborn Son back from the old man's arms and held Him tightly, how could she have anticipated what those words would mean?

She could not have known that before her Son turned three, she and Joseph and their toddler child would be forced to move to a foreign country, fleeing from the wrath of an insecure king who was jealous to protect his throne.

She could not have known that her Son who was pure goodness and love would be rejected and scorned by those He was sent to seek, serve, and save.

She could not have envisioned that three decades later, as a widow, she would watch as her firstborn was betrayed, falsely accused, tortured, and murdered.

Yes, a sword would pierce this mother's heart.

But though she didn't know the specific twists and turns her story would take, this young Jewish woman did evidence an awareness that her story was connected to a much larger Story that the God of history was writing. As the Holy Spirit came upon her, she somehow grasped that she was not the Protagonist of this story, that her life was being woven into a literary masterpiece God was writing for the display of His glory, the salvation of those who believe and, yes, the judgment of those who reject Him.

━━━⟳

"Trust and obey" was the default response of both Mary and Joseph to the unfolding of God's story for their lives. They heard His voice. They had no idea—nor do we—what the future would hold, but their confidence in the One who held the future was unassailable. So they said *Yes*. And in their obedience, they stepped into pivotal roles in the greater Story God was writing.

This couple's story was lived out at the hinge of human history.

From their vantage point in ancient Nazareth, they could not possibly have seen what is plain to us. That the baby to be born of Mary would split our calendar into BC and AD. That the longed-for redemption of God's people would come through this child, who was God incarnate.

The Holy One.

The good news of the gospel, wrapped in human flesh.

The One who came to redeem and rewrite the human story.

CHAPTER 15

Consummated

His Story

When that end cometh, we shall read . . .
the whole of God's purpose as one grand poem,
and there will not be one verse in it that has
a syllable too much, or a word too little; . . .
much less one that is erased,
but from beginning to end we shall see
the master-pen and the master-mind drawing forth
the glorious array of majestic thoughts.

CHARLES H. SPURGEON

When you go to a stage play, an usher usually hands you a bound program—a booklet—as you enter the theater. It's called the playbill, and it gives you a summary of the story you're about to see dramatized. With the help of a nice lady with a little flashlight, you find your row and your seat. And then, because you're early, you have time to do some reading.

You open the playbill. As you turn the pages, you learn who designed the set, something about the actors and actresses—

who they are, where they're from, their accomplishments—and (especially helpful if you happen to be watching an opera in a language you don't speak) a synopsis of each act.

> You can't tell what a novel or a play is about, where it's heading, or how it ends by randomly opening it to a page somewhere in the middle. To get the whole story, you have to read the whole book or script. So it is with God's Story.

The Bible is your Playbill tonight. It's your behind-the-scenes guide to a Story that was written before time began, when the stage was set for the grand Production. It tells us what we need to know about the Designer, the players, and the story line unfolding, both on the stage of human history and in heaven above.

So, with your Bible in hand, the play begins.

The curtain rises. A hush falls across the audience. You scoot to the edge of your seat. You don't want to miss anything. The stage is dark and empty. The Story opens.

In the beginning, God created . . . (Gen. 1:1)

At this point we learn who the Narrator is . . . the One who will tell the Story. His is the Voice we'll hear from start to finish:

And God said . . . (Gen. 1:3)

You can't tell what a novel or a play is about, where it's heading, or how it ends by randomly opening it to a page somewhere in the middle. To get the whole story, you have to read the whole book or script.

So it is with God's Story. The Bible has a beginning, a middle, and an end. This story line makes sense of our world and explains how we fit into God's eternal plan. It gives us a context, a grid through which to process hard things that come into our lives.

There are four main acts in this Story. Our Playbill tells us what to expect.

Part One

Act 1: Creation. God made this world—all of it, including the human race—to glorify and enjoy Him forever. He declared everything good and blessed all that He had created.

Act 2: Fall. Adam and Eve (and through them, all of their descendants) chose to rebel against this good God. The consequences of their declaration of independence were pervasive and tragic. The first couple were banished from Eden, the garden God had created for their pleasure. Their relationship with Him and with each other was fractured. The earth was placed under a curse—the curse of sin. Every form of injustice, hatred, violence, evil, strife, and abuse is borne out of sin in the heart, which ultimately leads to death. The brokenness caused by sin is seen everywhere in our world.

Intermission

Part Two

Act 3: Redemption. Even before sin made its appearance, God set in motion a plan to reconcile humans to Himself and to restore them to a place of blessing. He did so by sending His Son to this earth to live the sinless life we should have lived and to pay the price for sin with His own Life.

Act 4: New Creation. All of history is moving toward the cap-stone—the consummation—of His Story. Christ will return to this earth, bringing eternal judgment to His enemies and eternal salvation to those who belong to Him. He will create a new heaven and earth—free from all sin and suffering—and will reign forever without a rival.

In part one—what we know as the Old Testament—we see God's people rebelling against Him. Time and again He extends His mercy and pardon. The people repent. But time and again they sin. Time and time again.

All along, God hints at the final two Acts. He promises to send a Rescuer, one who will perfectly fulfill the divine law that all of humanity has broken. One who will succeed where human-kind has failed. One who will redeem our brokenness and fallen-ness and reconcile us to the Father.

We are given glimpses of this coming One throughout the pages of the Old Testament. He is (and was, and will be)

- the Offspring of the woman (Gen. 3:15)

- the Star of Jacob (Num. 24:17)

- the Prophet like Moses (Deut. 18:15)

- the Commander of the army of the Lord (Josh. 5:14)

- the Kinsman-Redeemer (Ruth 3:9)

- the risen and returning Redeemer (Job 19:25)

- the Good Shepherd (Ps. 23:1)

- the Chief among ten thousand (Song of Songs 5:10 NKJV)

- the Sun of righteousness, risen with healing in His wings (Mal. 4:2)

- and so much more!

Yet year after passing year, the people wait, generation after weary generation. Where is He? When will He come? *Will* He ever come?

The theater lights brighten. We stand at our places, and intermission begins. But this is no ordinary interval.

This suspension of the drama lasts four hundred years. The stage stands dark and dormant. The Narrator is silent.

Prophets are no more. Priests continue their routines, but the promises of a new day dawning grow faint in their memory. God's people live through generation after generation of celestial blackout.

Then the lights in the vestibule flicker. The long wait is over. Part two is about to begin.

You return to your seat and look again at the Playbill. Somehow, you'd overlooked the name of the next act. Now you see it printed right there: *redemption.*

This is the act where God enters the story personally through the birth of an infant and brings it to a climax with a death and a resurrection. Though long foretold, these plot developments took everyone (except God, of course) by surprise. And they changed everything!

Long lay the world in sin and error pining
Till he appeared and the soul felt its worth.
A thrill of hope—the weary soul rejoices,
For yonder breaks a new and glorious morn![1]

Paradise (creation), *Paradise Lost* (the fall), and *Paradise Restored* (redemption and new creation)—these are the Big Ideas of God's Story. But right now, we are living in a transition between Paradise Lost and Paradise Restored. We still suffer from the effects of the fall, and so often it seems that evil prevails. But thankfully, through Christ, our faithful, all-powerful God is in the process of redeeming and making all things new.

> We still suffer from the effects of the fall, and so often it seems that evil prevails. But thankfully, through Christ, our faithful, all-powerful God is in the process of redeeming and making all things new.

There are pages and chapters in our lives that seem to make little sense. They may even seem heartless and cruel—certainly not the kind of Story a good God would write.

If we look only at the tiny slice of reality in which we live, we could conclude—as many do—that our world is hopelessly insane, and we are merely victims of random fate or of a malevolent god who is unworthy of our trust and loyalty. For sure, we would have no reason for hope, peace, or joy.

But in God's Word we find a backstory that shows us what once was and how things got to where they are today. And there we discover a God who is faithful, whose Story cannot be thwarted, and who is always working to accomplish His good, eternal plan, using even twisted human actions and circumstances to bring glory to Himself in the end. And there we find promises of a bright and certain future that awaits us.

Do you ever find yourself reading a novel and wanting to skip ahead to the end to find out what happens? The plot is complex and scary, each page a nail-biter. It seems the good guys are being overpowered and crushed by the bad guys. "How does this all turn out?" you want to know. You're eager to find out whether and how the problems get resolved, the mysteries solved, whether there will be a happy ending.

Sometimes that's what we want in life—to be able to look ahead and know what will happen. Will the Lord ever send me a mate? Will my marriage ever be happy again? Will my prodigal child return home? Will I be able to find a job? Will my sister survive this diagnosis? Will my elderly, unbelieving dad ever trust in Christ? What will my death be like?

We want to skip over the long, hard chapters, with all their pain and problems, and get right to the end. Of course, that's not possible.

> In His Word we discover a God who is faithful, whose Story cannot be thwarted, and who is always working to accomplish His good, eternal plan, using even twisted human actions and circumstances to bring glory to Himself in the end.

However, in His Word, God tells us just enough about the end of the Story to give us hope and courage to face what lies between here and there . . . now and then.

It's hard to overestimate the importance of a strong ending. A good conclusion makes all that has transpired meaningful. Otherwise, we're left disappointed.

Sometimes, the ending is not at all what you expected. Back when you were in school, you may have read some short stories by William Sydney Porter (1862–1910), better known by his pen name, "O. Henry." His stories are set in his own day and often deal with ordinary people. Among his most famous stories is *The Gift of the Magi*, which has been retold in countless forms and variations over the past hundred years.

The signature feature of O. Henry's short stories is their surprise endings. *Whoa,* you think when you turn to the final page, *I didn't expect that!* And then, suddenly, everything makes sense. As the reader, you're rewarded for your patience and satisfied that the outcome is as it should be.

In the end, God's Story will be like that. It will be far better than anything we ever imagined, surprising and delighting all those who have trusted Him. But the end will also shock and terrify all those who thought they could ignore or defy Him and get away with it. It will be far worse than anything they ever imagined.

Denouement is a word I (Nancy) have loved since I first learned it in a high school literature class. It's a French word that refers to the final part of a story, the part where all the plot strands come together and everything is explained or resolved. It's usually the moment when everything becomes clear and the final outcome is revealed.

As the writer of a story, you don't want to give away all the developments of the plot too early. You want to keep readers with you right up to the very end. Kind of like saving the biggest, brightest, and best fireworks for the end of the Independence Day show. Or Jesus making the best wine at the end of the wedding feast in Cana.

But the final act of God's Story will eclipse the ending of every other story ever told.

Deus ex machina is a term from ancient Greek theater that literally means "the god from the machine." This device was sometimes used by ancient playwrights when they couldn't figure out how to resolve a complex or hopeless plot. They would use machinery to fly a "god" onto the stage, sometimes on a cloud, to solve all the problems and dramatically announce "The End." Presto. *Fine.* Curtain down.

The term is now used to refer to the type of story ending "in which an outside force determines the outcome rather than the actions and decisions taken by the characters." [2] At the last second, out of nowhere, something or someone suddenly appears, wipes out the bad guys, rescues the good guys, resolves the conflict, and fixes everything that is wrong.

Writing teachers agree that *deus ex machina* is *not* the way to end a story. It's considered lazy—a shortcut to solve complex problems and bring about resolution. And . . . it's just not plausible.

But this dramatic device gives us a sense of how God's Story will end. *Deus ex machina* reminds us of one of the most dramatic, climactic passages in all of God's Word. It's found near the end of the Bible and describes the outcome of the final battle when God will deal the decisive blow to all rebellion and unrighteousness.

> Then I saw heaven opened, and behold, a white horse!
> The one sitting on it is called Faithful and True, and in

righteousness he judges and makes war. . . .

He is clothed in a robe dipped in blood, and the name by which he is called is The Word of God.

And the armies of heaven, arrayed in fine linen, white and pure, were following him on white horses.

From his mouth comes a sharp sword with which to strike down the nations, and he will rule them with a rod of iron. He will tread the winepress of the fury of the wrath of God the Almighty.

On his robe and on his thigh he has a name written, King of kings and Lord of lords. (Rev. 19:11–16)

Talk about God (not "a god") flying in to right every wrong on this sinful earth! This is the beginning of the ending—and then the New Creation comes to pass. All things are made right and new. Paradise is restored, never to be lost again.

This is the denouement of God's Story—the satisfying ending and explanation to which we look forward even while we experience the suffering, loss, and brokenness of life in this "already, but not yet" state. This is the hope to which we anchor our souls. The promise on which we stake our lives.

Hallelujah! It is finished! Amen.

Come, Lord Jesus!

CHAPTER 16

You Can Trust God...
You Really Can

Your Story

Your story is a biography of
wisdom and grace written by another.
Every turn he writes into your story is right.
Every twist of the plot is for the best.
Every new character or unexpected event
is a tool of his grace.
Each new chapter advances his purpose.

PAUL TRIPP

*I*magine that you're watching your favorite sports team play in a championship game. The game is down to the wire and the two teams are neck and neck. Normally you'd be on the edge of your seat, biting your nails, holding your breath, yelling "No way!" when a bad call or play is made.

But not this time. Instead you grab a snack, sit back in your favorite chair, put your feet up, and enjoy the game. You're not in the least bit anxious. Why?

Because you're watching a replay of the game. And you've

already heard the outcome—you know that your team *won*. That totally changes the way you watch the game. You know how it's going to end. No need to be stressed.

Of course, life is far more serious than a game. At times it's more like a war! But for those who are in Christ, there is no need to fret, no matter what frustrating calls or plays may be made.

Why?

Because we know Who wins! And that's why we can keep on trusting God, even in those times when our story isn't unfolding the way we had hoped it would or thought it should.

⌐⟋⟍⟍⟍⟍⟍⟍⟍⟍

We first heard Tayler Beede's story from her dad, Scott Lindsay, who is a friend of ours; we've since followed it on a couple of blogs she writes for.

Tayler had dreams and carefully crafted plans for her future with her husband, Kyle. And they didn't include the loss of a baby and a brain tumor, all before the age of twenty-two. That's not what she ever hoped or prayed for.

But that's what her story looks like so far. And she has been in a journey to let go of those dreams she once held on to so tightly. She writes,

> If I truly trust God with my life, that means I trust him with every aspect. Each and every word, sentence, and chapter. Even when I feel like I can't bear to flip the page and see what happens next....
>
> It's all part of what makes our faith so scary and yet so beautiful. And because of our faith in Christ, we know that in the end he will redeem all of the scary and seemingly hopeless patches.[1]

⌐⟋⟍⟍⟍⟍⟍⟍⟍⟍

"So, tell us your story."

This is something we often say to people, even complete strangers with whom we've just struck up a conversation.

When we ask you this question, we're not talking about the stories you post on Instagram, meant to entertain or impress. We want to hear your story—who you really are and how you got there; your longings and burdens, joys and trials, struggles and challenges; what keeps you up at night and what gets you up in the morning.

In response, you may think, *There's nothing special about me or my story. Seriously? Why would anyone care?*

Oh, but we really do care about your story. And even more, we believe that God cares about it—about the story He's in the process of shaping through your life.

But my story is such a mess! you may be thinking. *And you've been telling me I can trust God to write it. How could His story for my life (or the life of someone I love) include*

> We'd like to experience the benefits and blessings of suffering . . . without suffering. We admire others' stories of grace through fire, but we want our own stories to be fireproof. But God loves us too much to let us have that kind of life.

- never knowing who my dad was and being abandoned by my mom when I was two;

- hearing my wife say, "I've found somebody new";

- having an unknown intruder break into my apartment and rape me during my senior year of college;

- suffering multiple, painful miscarriages and never being able to carry a child to term;

- watching my child walk out the door in open rebellion . . . not knowing where she is or if I'll ever see her again;

- sitting in a doctor's office and hearing, "The tests are back. You have MS";

- or _____ (you fill in the blank)?

These are chapters in a life story for which there are no simple explanations.

Being followers of Christ doesn't make us immune to pain and heartache. In fact, some of the most faithful men and women in Scripture suffered greatly. And that's not a coincidence.

~~~

For over thirty years of Sunday school teaching, I (Robert) chose the same Bible text on the first Sunday of every new year. This familiar passage in Hebrews 12 speaks of a "great . . . cloud of witnesses" that surrounds us as we run the race God has assigned to us (v. 1). When we grow weary from running, when we want to call it quits, this vast crowd in the stands encourages us to press on.

And just who are these witnesses? We can read about some of them in the previous chapter of Hebrews, where we find a long list of heroes of the faith. We admire these Old Testament men and women and their accomplishments. We want to emulate their faith. Yet most of their stories had pages and chapters none of us would wish to have as part of our story. In fact, many had what we might consider tragic endings—not at all the way we think the stories of God's faithful servants should end:

> Some were tortured, refusing to accept release, so that they might rise again to a better life. Others suffered mocking and flogging, and even chains and imprisonment. They were stoned, they were sawn in two, they were killed with the sword. They went about in skins of sheep and goats, destitute, afflicted, mistreated—of whom the world was not worthy— wandering about in deserts and mountains, and in dens and caves of the earth. (Heb. 11:35–38)

So how did these faithful saints endure? What kept them from throwing in the towel?

For starters, they knew that what they could see was not the end of the story. They knew God had more in store for them just ahead. Holding fast to that promise enabled them to persevere in hope, even when their suffering did not end in this life.

> These all died in faith, not having received the things promised, but having seen them and greeted them from afar, and having acknowledged that they were strangers and exiles on the earth. For people who speak thus make it clear that they are seeking a homeland. . . . They desire a better country, that is, a heavenly one. Therefore God is not ashamed to be called their God, for he has prepared for them a city. (vv. 13–16)

They did not see the whole story during their lifetime here on earth. Nor can we see the whole story during our brief stay here.

These men and women have gone before us. They have already run their race. Their stories are finished. But ours are still being written. So, the writer of Hebrews urges, "Let us run with endurance the race that is set before us" (Heb. 12:1). Our spiritual ancestors ran their race; now it's time for us to run ours. And that takes perseverance, staying power, steadfastness.

How do we develop those qualities? Through trials, testing, tribulation. No exceptions. No shortcuts.

⌐⌐

Through the course of writing this book, many dear friends (and a few strangers) have opened up their hearts to us. They have trusted us with some of the darkest, hardest chapters, the most painful memories, of their stories. Our conversations with them have been holy ground for us. A sacred stewardship.

> God's Story is about far more than just giving us an uneventful joyride to heaven. It is about His kingdom coming and His will being done on earth— in us!—as it is in heaven. It is about preparing and fitting us for eternity.

In each case we have marveled at the endurance these men and women have exhibited during the most demanding, difficult stretches of the race set before them. And we have been in awe as we have observed the incredibly rich, sweet fruit that has been borne in their lives—not in spite of, but because of, their pain and loss.

We've come away from these exchanges reminded that affliction really does do everything Scripture says it does—in us and through us:

We know that affliction produces endurance, endurance produces proven character, and proven character produces hope. This hope will not disappoint us. (Rom. 5:3–5 CSB)

In the midst of the fire, these friends have clung to His promises; and they have not been disappointed. They have never been forsaken by God (though it may have felt that way at times). To the contrary, they have experienced His nearness and dearness as never before. And strange as it may seem, most have told us that they would not trade their experience—pain and all—for anything this world can offer.

We'd all like to have that kind of fruit in our lives. We want to be closer to God, to have strong faith and unsinkable peace, to swim in the depths of His love and grace, to have proven, godly character, and to be hope-filled people. But we'd prefer to have all of that without going through what they've been through.

We'd like to experience the benefits and blessings of suffering... without suffering.

We admire others' stories of grace through fire, but we want our own stories to be fireproof.

We know that diamonds are formed in the dark places of the earth under intense pressure through prolonged periods of time. But we want the outcome—sparkling, precious gems—without the process.

If we were to write our own stories or the stories of our closest family and friends, we'd opt for sunny skies and smooth sailing and skip the dreary, stormy days. Page after page would include what's familiar and predictable, with as few changes and surprises as possible. We'd like to float down the gentle, shallow waters of the lazy river of life, avoiding any currents or rapids that we can't handle on our own.

Bottom line? We'd pen a narrative in which we don't (really) need God except perhaps as a cosmic Blessing Dispenser.

But God loves us too much to let us have that kind of life.

God loves you too much for that.

━━⁀

"You do not have a story until something goes wrong."

Master storyteller and bestselling novelist Steven James's pithy advice for would-be writers also applies to the story God is writing in our lives. As James puts it:

> At its heart, a story is about a person dealing with tension, and tension is created by unfulfilled desire. Without forces of antagonism, without setbacks, without a crisis event that initiates the action, you have no story.[2]

God's Story is about far more than just giving us an uneventful joyride to heaven. It is about His kingdom coming and His will being done on earth—in us!—as it is in heaven. It is about preparing and fitting us for eternity. And it is about changing us, growing us up from immature, self-absorbed, idol-worshiping, whining, sinning brats into mature, Christ-absorbed, God-exalting, grateful, obedient followers and friends. Like all good stories, it is about *transformation*.

Steven James explains:

> Plot is the journey toward transformation. . . . At its most basic level, a story is a transformation unveiled—either the transformation of a situation or, most commonly, the transformation of a character."[3]

The determining factor in the process of change is how the character responds to the plot. James points out that every story has two kinds of characters—what he calls "pebble people" and "putty people." Here's how he describes the difference:

> If you take a pebble and throw it against a wall, it'll bounce off the wall unchanged. But if you throw a ball of putty against a wall hard enough, it will change shape. . . .

> When you throw [a putty person] into the crisis of the
> story, he is forever changed. . . . He'll always be a different
> shape at the end of the story than he was at the beginning. [4]

Pebble people remain the same no matter what happens to and around them. They are not particularly interesting. More important, in God's Story, pebble people tend to be resistant to what He wants to do with their lives.

But *putty people* say to God, "You are the Potter; I am the clay (see Jer. 18:1–6). Change me, mold me, and if necessary break and remake me . . . into the person you created me to be."

One such "putty person" has been forever altered by her suffering, and in turn has become an instrument of grace and transformation in countless other lives, including our own.

On a hot summer day in 1967, a seventeen-year-old girl dove into the Chesapeake Bay near her home in Maryland. She misjudged the depth of the water and hit bottom, breaking her neck. In an instant this carefree teen became a quadriplegic. She would be confined to a wheelchair for the rest of her life, unable to use her arms or legs and often in chronic pain. She would never be the same again. A "tragic accident," most would call it.

> For every child of God, in every circumstance, the best really is yet to come.

And that's how our dear friend **Joni Eareckson Tada** viewed it herself over the next two years of hospital stays and rehab as she battled intense anger, depression, suicidal thoughts, doubts about her faith, and fear about her future. She recalls:

> I wanted to trust God, but I was still anxious. . . . If God
> allowed my accident to happen at such a young age, an
> accident that left me a quadriplegic, then what might He
> do next? What else would He do? [5]

Then God in His Providence brought a young man named Steve Estes into Joni's life. Steve wasn't put off by Joni's tough questions, and he patiently helped her find solid footing for her heart, even as she was in great physical pain, figuring out how to function with her immobile body. After she got out of the hospital, he met weekly with her and a couple of other friends whose faith had also been shaken by her quadriplegia.

With an open Bible, Steve showed them that God hates human suffering, but that our suffering fits into a "grand mosaic"—a bigger picture that is clear to Him but is largely concealed to us. On this side of eternity, we can't see how this picture will turn out in the end. But He knows the outcome, and He has promised it will end in great good for us and glory for Himself.

When she is asked to pinpoint what one thing changed her whole perspective after her accident, Joni says without hesitation that it was the night when Steve turned to her and said, "Joni, sometimes God permits what He hates to accomplish that which He loves." [6]

That sentence turned a lightbulb on for Joni. She saw, for example, how God permitted His own Son to be put to death, hating the cruelty and injustice while loving what would be accomplished by the cross—salvation for all who would believe.

> In the same way, God hated my spinal cord injury—He
> allowed that awful, awful accident to happen which resulted
> in my permanent paralysis. But, He delighted [in] how my
> accident fit into a grand mosaic of good not only for me, but
> for so many other people with disabilities—people whom
> I've had a chance to help. . . . Yes, God will permit things that

He hates, but He'll allow those things so that something that
He loves can be accomplished.[7]

What has God permitted to be a part of your story that seems
inconsistent with His goodness and love? Might He be allowing
that "thing" He hates in order to accomplish that which He loves?

As we were discussing this theme with our friend and film
producer, Stephen Kendrick, he put it this way: "God likes to use
really, really bad things to do really, really good things."

As we were working on this chapter, I (Nancy) ran into a friend
whose husband, a man in his early fifties, is in advanced stages of
early-onset Alzheimer's and now requires full-time medical care. It
has been a grueling journey for both of them, and it's not over. I
could hear the weariness in my friend's voice when I talked with
her. From our finite, limited perspective, this makes no sense at all.

We know that suffering is an unavoidable part of every human's story. It should not surprise us. But when it comes to us,
how do we deal with it? How do we persevere? When massive
waves are swirling around us, how do we keep from going under?

Getting a right perspective is critical—lifting our eyes *up-
ward* to God rather than *outward* to our circumstances or *inward*
to ourselves. Counseling our hearts according to truth. Realign-
ing our thoughts and emotions according to His Story.

In 1895, a South African pastor, teacher, and writer named
Andrew Murray (1828–1917) was preaching at large Christian
conferences in England. In physical pain from an injury sustained
a few years earlier (thrown from a cart while traveling and ministering)[8] and having just received some discouraging criticism
from a well-known person, the exhausted Murray opted to stay
in bed one Sunday morning. But rather than wallowing in dis-

couragement or indulging melancholia, he decided to write some notes for his own encouragement.

At the top of the paper he wrote, "In Time of Trouble Say . . ." Then he penned the following, counseling his own heart with the truth:

> *First*, He brought me here; it is by His will I am in this strait place: in that fact I will rest.
>
> *Next*, He will keep me here in His love, and give me grace to behave as His child.
>
> *Then*, He will make the trial a blessing, teaching me the lessons He intends me to learn, and working in me the grace He means to bestow.
>
> *Last*, In His good time He can bring me out again—how and when He knows.
>
> Let me say I am here,
>
> 1) By God's appointment.
> 2) In His keeping.
> 3) Under His training.
> 4) For His time.[9]

We can't remind ourselves of these truths too often. In fact, you might want to copy Murray's words and put them somewhere where you can review them whenever you are in a "time of trouble." And here's one of my (Nancy's) most frequently shared quotes, by pastor and author Warren Wiersbe, that you may want to add to Andrew Murray's affirmation:

> When God puts us in the furnace, He always keeps His eye on the clock and His hand on the thermostat.[10]

Always.

Never forget that God loves you. He is watching over you. He knows how long and how much you can endure. What you're going through will not last forever. And whatever kind of suffering you may be facing—whether you have something you don't want or you're wanting something you don't have—this is the kind of heavenly, right-sized perspective that will give you grace, courage, and stamina to carry on.

So first, look up. Be strengthened by a vision of God's Providence and purposes.

And then . . . look ahead. Find hope by holding fast to His promises. This is what kept **Andrea and Josh Smith** moving forward in the race God had for them.

Andrea was a runner, had always exercised regularly, and, as far as she knew, was perfectly healthy. Then, in 2013, she was diagnosed with stage 4 cancer. She had a large tumor in her chest cavity, surrounding her heart, as well as a tumor in her liver. She and her pastor-husband, Josh, and their four young girls could not have imagined the incredibly long, hard road they would face in the months ahead. Because of the tumor around her heart, surgery was not an option at first. Over the next nine months, she

> Not only can you trust God to write your story; you can also be sure that, in the end, He will *right* your story! Every sin or injustice committed against you, every sinful or foolish choice you made, everything you feared would permanently mark and mar your life . . . one day it will all be made right.

underwent six hundred hours of chemo, four spinal infusions to get chemo to her brain, a major surgery, and twenty-four rounds of radiation. Andrea was extremely sick for a very long time.

But Andrea and Josh understood that God was writing their story. Throughout their journey, Josh sent out periodic email updates to those of us who were carrying them on our hearts. Regardless of how discouraging the latest report was, his updates were always signed,

The best is yet to come.

In God's mercy, Andrea recovered—supernaturally, it appears. But for a long while, this couple had no idea whether they would experience a positive outcome this side of heaven. They were not sustained by any guarantee that Andrea would be made well in this life, but by the confidence that in the end all would be well.

As I (Nancy) followed Josh and Andrea's story, I was struck by the recurring reminder in each update that, for every child of God, in every circumstance, the best really is yet to come. Our hope for a joyful future is not in healing or doctors or answers or solutions to our problems—but in the assurance that . . .

> Eye has not seen, nor ear heard,
> Nor have entered into the heart of man
> The things which God has prepared for those who love him.
> (1 Cor. 2:9 NKJV)

Remember that you don't know how the last chapter reads. At the moment, you're in the middle of a paragraph, in the middle of a page, in the middle of a chapter, in the middle of a whole book. You can trust God not just for the paragraph you're in, but for every paragraph and chapter to come. And what's more, not only can you trust God to write your story; you can also be sure that, in the end, He will *right* your story!

What hope that should give you between now and then! Every sin or injustice committed against you, every sinful or foolish choice you made, everything you feared would permanently mark and mar your life, all that was confusing and convoluted and corrupt . . . one day it will all be made right.

In the light of that promise, we can pray, in the words of Scotty Smith:

> *Grant us fresh grace to wait upon you*
> *for the future and hope to which you have called us. . . .*
> *Turn our whines into worship,*
> *our daily carping into carpe diem,*
> *and our frets into faith.* [11]

Amen.

How have you found God to be faithful
in unexpected or difficult chapters of your life?
Share your story *on your favorite social media platform.*
#TrustGodToWriteYourStory

With Gratitude

*T*he initial idea for *You Can Trust God to Write Your Story* was born from a conversation with a publisher that didn't turn out to be the publisher. In 2016, Christian publishing's premier gift-book producers, Countryman Books, spoke with us about sharing our unusual love story in print. Over time the concept changed and the length of the manuscript increased. When all was said and done, it didn't prove to be the right fit for a gift-book format, so we agreed to move in a different direction. Thank you, Laura Minchew, Jack Countryman, LeeEric Fesco, and Kristen Parrish for getting the ball rolling and for your grace in this process.

Our friends at Moody Publishers picked up the project and agreed to publish this book. Sometimes the word *friend* is used without much thought or meaning. But in this case it's more appropriate than you can imagine. The men and women who oversee and lead Moody Publishers are, in fact, dear friends: Greg Thornton, Paul Santhouse, Randall Payleitner, Judy Dunagan, Connor Sterchi, Erik Peterson, Janis Todd, Grace Park, Ashley Torres, and Kate Warren, among many others. Our thanks go out to each one of you.

Once we had finished the first draft of the manuscript, we called another longtime friend, Anne Christian Buchanan, who in the parlance of book publishing could be considered a licensed book doctor. Anne's technical and wordsmithing skills, coupled with her grace-filled wisdom, patiently took our manuscript to the next level. Thank you, Anne!

We are also thankful for Erik Wolgemuth, our agent and advocate for this project, as well as our other colleagues at Wolgemuth & Associates. What a joy it is to work with these capable men.

A big thank-you to our ministry associates at Revive Our Hearts, whose faithful support, encouragement, and prayers made it possible for us to undertake this project.

Our deepest gratitude goes to the people whose stories made their way into this book. Some of our meetings with them took place in person. Most happened on the phone. At the end of each conversation, we looked at each other with a fresh sense of wonder, realizing what a gift they had given us in telling us their story and what a stewardship was ours to carefully share with you what we had just heard.

Finally, we are thankful for the Providence of our heavenly Father, who loves us, goes before us, directs our steps, and is faithfully writing each of our stories. How hopeless our lives would be without Him . . . and how rich they are under His loving care.

Notes

Introduction

Epigraph: Quoted in Ryan and Tina Essmaker, "Scott and Vik Harrison,"
interview published on The Great Discontent, February 12, 2013,
https://thegreatdiscontent.com/interview/scott-and-vik-harrison.

1. In a lovely bookend, God's Story closes in a garden city—the heavenly
   Eden. See Revelation 2:7 (the English word paradise comes from a
   Greek word meaning "park" or "garden") and 22:1–2.

Chapter 1: Of Birds, Flowers, and You: Living under Providence

Epigraph: Donna Kelderman, *Seasons of the Heart: A Year of Devotions
from One Generation of Women to Another* (Grand Rapids:
Reformation Heritage Books, 2013), August 17.

1. Noah Webster, *American Dictionary of the English Language*,
   Webster's Dictionary 1828—Online Edition, s.v. "providence,"
   http://webstersdictionary1828.com/Dictionary/providence.

2. Charlie Dates (@CharlieDates), "I'm amazed at how, on a bumpy
   flight, the pilot's voice is calm and assured when addressing the
   passengers. . . ." Twitter. January 9, 2019, http://www.twipu.com/
   CharlieDates/tweet/1083043266407292934.

3. "Those who wait for me shall not be put to shame" (Isa. 49:23) can
   also be translated "anyone who trusts in me will not be disappointed"
   (ESV). See Blue Letter Bible Lexicon, s.v. buwsh (Strong's H954),
   Blue Letter Bible website, version 3, https://www.blueletterbible.org/
   lang/lexicon/lexicon.cfm?Strongs=H854&t=ESV.

Chapter 2: **Chosen: Esther's Story**

Epigraph: Tony Evans, *Pathways: From Providence to Purpose* (Nashville: B&H, 2019), 166.

1. "Who Was Haman the Agagite," Got Questions, accessed January 19, 2019, https://www.gotquestions.org/Haman-the-Agagite.html. But see also "Was Haman an Agagite," Bible Hermeneutics Stack Exchange, accessed January 19, 2019, https://hermeneutics.stackexchange.com/questions/8193/was-haman-an-agagite.

2. To this day, the festive holiday of Purim, named for the "Pur" that Haman cast to determine the date of his planned genocide, is recognized among Jews as the day Haman was hanged and the Jewish nation was spared.

3. Maltbie D. Babcock, "This Is My Father's World" (1901), Hymntime, accessed January 20, 2019, http://www.hymntime.com/tch/htm/t/i/s/tismyfw.htm.

Chapter 3: **Graced: Our Story**

Epigraph: F. B. Meyer, *Paul: A Servant of Jesus Christ* (1897; repr., CreateSpace, 2017), 23.

1. Katherine Hankey, "I Love to Tell the Story" (1866), Hymnary.org, accessed January 19, 2019, https://hymnary.org/text/i_love_to_tell_the_story_of_unseen_thing.

2. These lines are from a longer poem by the English missionary C. T. Studd (1860–1931). The entirety of this public domain poem can be found at Joshua Van Der Merwe, "Only One Life: A Poem by C. T. Studd," *With One Aim* (blog), accessed January 19, 2019, https://joshuavandermerwe.wordpress.com/2014/01/23/only-one-life-a-poem-by-c-t-studd/.

3. "Unexpected Grace: Nancy and Robert's Story," Revive Our Hearts, 2015, video, 16:01, https://www.reviveourhearts.com/about/nancy-demoss-wolgemuth/nancy-and-robert/.

Chapter 4: You Can Trust God When Your Marriage Is in Trouble

Epigraph: Larry Crabb, *The Pressure's Off: There's a New Way to Live*, 1st ed. (Colorado Springs: WaterBrook, 2002), 76.

1. Jerry Bridges, *31 Days Toward Trusting God* (Carol Stream, IL: NavPress/Tyndale House, 2013), 50 (Day 11).

2. You can see a profile video of Lorna's testimony on the Revive Our Hearts website. See "Lorna's Story of Forgiveness (Profile Video)," Revive Our Hearts, posted October 11, 2008, https://www .reviveourhearts.com/events/true-woman-08/lornas-story-forgiveness-profile-video/.

Chapter 5: You Can Trust God When You Long for a Mate

Epigraph: Elisabeth Elliot, *The Path of Loneliness: Finding Your Way through the Wilderness to God* (Grand Rapids: Revell, 2007), 32.

1. Elisabeth Elliot, *Suffering Is Never for Nothing* (Nashville: B&H, 2019), 9.

2. Biographical details compiled from "About Elisabeth," Elisabeth Elliot, accessed January 20, 2018, http://www.elisabethelliot.org/ about.html; Sam Roberts, "Elisabeth Elliot, Tenacious Missionary in Face of Tragedy, Dies at 88," *New York Times*, June 18, 2015, https:// www.nytimes.com/2015/06/18/us/elisabeth-elliot-tenacious-missionary-to-ecuador-dies-at-88.html; and other sources.

3. You'll note that those we've selected are women. That is not to say that men don't wrestle at times with an unfulfilled longing for marriage. But in our experience, this is a more common struggle for women, especially those who believe guys have a God-given responsibility to initiate a relationship and who may feel there is little they can do to change their marital status.

4. Nancy Leigh DeMoss, *Choosing Gratitude: Your Journey to Joy* (Chicago: Moody, 2011), 23, emphasis added.

5. Bethany Beal, "Single and Surviving Wedding Season," blog post on Lies Young Women Believe, July 18, 2018, http://www .liesyoungwomenbelieve.com/single-surviving-wedding-season/ ?doing_wp_cron=1532100383.1958589553833007812500.

Chapter 6: You Can Trust God When You're Pressed Financially
Epigraph: H.B. Charles Jr., *It Happens after Prayer: Biblical Motivation for Believing Prayer* (Chicago: Moody, 2013), 40.
1. Arthur S. DeMoss, *God's Secret of Success* (West Palm Beach, FL: Arthur S. DeMoss Foundation, 2002, orig. pub. 1980), 4.

Chapter 7: Redeemed: Naomi and Ruth's Story
Epigraph: Jon Bloom, "When It Seems Like God Did You Wrong," Desiring God, April 25, 2014, https://www.desiringgod .org/articles/when-it-seems-like-god-did-you-wrong.

Chapter 8: You Can Trust God When You Lose Your Health
Epigraph: Amy Carmichael, "Tender Toward Others," in *KJV Devotional Bible* (Peabody, MA: Hendrickson Bibles, 2011), 1486 (Hebrews 12:15).
1. Blue Letter Bible Lexicon, s.v. skolops (Strong's G4647), Blue Letter Bible website, version 3, https://www.blueletterbible.org/lang/lexicon/lexicon.cfm?Strongs=G4647&t=ESV.
2. The quotations in this section are taken from Colleen's emails and are used by permission.
3. Joshua Rogers, "My Baby Nephew Was Dying and His Mother's Response Was Unforgettable," Fox News, July 14, 2018, http://www.foxnews.com/opinion/2018/07/14/my-baby-nephew-was-dying-and-his-mothers-response-was-unforgettable.html.
4. Ibid.
5. Ibid.

Chapter 9: You Can Trust God When You've Been Sinned Against
Epigraph: Eric Liddell, *The Disciplines of the Christian Life* (London: SPCK Publishing, 2009), 121–22.
1. All names in this chapter have been changed, along with identifying details.
2. James 4:6.

Chapter 10: Sent: Joseph's Story

Epigraph: John Flavel, *The Mystery of Providence* (Apollo, PA: Ichthus Publications, 2014), 45. Originally published in 1824 under the title *Divine Conduct; or The Mystery of Providence.*

1. This is indicated by Genesis 40:3–4, which uses the same "captain of the guard" title to refer to the man in charge of Joseph's prison. See Herbert Carl Leupold, Exposition of Genesis: Volume 1, commentary on Genesis 40:1–23, Bible Hub, accessed January 23, 2019, https://biblehub.com/library/leupold/exposition_of_genesis_volume_1/chapter_xl.htm.

Chapter 11: You Can Trust God When Your Child Breaks Your Heart

Epigraph: Robert J. Morgan, *Prayers and Promises for Worried Parents: Hope for Your Prodigal. Help for You* (Nashville: Howard, 20003), 1–2.

Chapter 12: You Can Trust God When You Lose a Loved One

1. Thomas O. Chisolm, "Great Is Thy Faithfulness" (1923), Hymnary .org, accessed January 23, 2019, https://hymnary.org/text/great_is_thy_faithfulness_o_god_my_father.

2. George Müller, *Autobiography of George Müller, or A Million and a Half in Answer to Prayer*, comp. G. Fred. Bergin (London: Pickering & Inglis, 1929), 431.

3. George Müller, *A Narrative of Some of the Lord's Dealing with George Müller, Written by Himself, Jehovah Magnified:* Addresses by George Müller, Complete and Unabridged, Volume 2 (Muskegon, MI: Dust and Ashes, 2003), 392–93.

Chapter 13: You Can Trust God When You're Facing Death

Epigraph: Timothy Keller, *Walking with God through Pain and Suffering* (New York: Penguin, 2013), 44.

1. John Bunyan, *The Pilgrim's Progress: Complete and Unabridged*, Hendrickson Christian Classics (Peabody, MA: Hendrickson, 2004), 129.

2. *The Lord of the Rings: The Return of the King* (2003) Quotes, IMDb (International Movie Database website), accessed January 25, 2019, https://www.imdb.com/title/tt0167260/quotes/?tab=qt&ref_=tt_trv_qu.

3. Bunyan, *Pilgrim's Progress*, 133.

4. Interview recorded at staff chapel service for Life Action Ministries/ Revive Our Hearts on February 14, 2018.

Chapter 14: Surprised: Mary and Joseph's Story

Epigraph: Francis Chan with Danae Yankoski, *Crazy Love: Overwhelmed by a Relentless God*, 2nd ed. (Colorado Springs: David C. Cook, 2013), 122.

1. Other Bible translations call Joseph "a good man" (CEV), "a righteous man" (NASB), a man "faithful to the law" (NIV).

Chapter 15: Consummated: His Story

Epigraph: Charles Haddon Spurgeon, "A Feast for Faith," Sermon No. 711, delivered September 16, 1866 at Metropolitan Tabernacle, The Spurgeon Center for Biblical Preaching at Midwestern Seminary, accessed February 18, 2109, https://www.spurgeon.org/resource-library/sermons/a-feast-for-faith#flipbook/.

1. Text by Placide Cappeau (1847), tr. John S. Dwight, *Baptist Hymnal* (Nashville: LifeWay Reference, 2008), 194, reproduced in Hymnary .org, accessed January 25, 2019, https://hymnary.org/text/o_holy_ night_the_stars_are_brightly_shin#authority_media_flexscores.

2. Glen C. Strathy, "Effective Story Endings," How to Write a Book Now, accesssed January 25, 2019, https://www.how-to-write-a-book-now .com/story-endings.html.

Chapter 16: You Can Trust God . . . You Really Can: Your Story

Epigraph: Paul David Tripp, *New Morning Mercies: A Daily Gospel Devotional* (Wheaton, IL: Crossway, 2014), 203.

1. Taylor Beede, "Trusting God to Write Your Story," Girlfriends in God, November 27, 2017, http://girlfriendsingod.com/trusting-god-write-story/.

2. Steven James, "The 5 Essential Story Ingredients," guest column, *Writer's Digest*, May 9, 2014, http://www.writersdigest.com/online-editor/the-5-essential-story-ingredients.

3. Ibid.

4. Ibid.

5. Joni Eareckson Tada, "God Permits What He Hates," transcript of radio program #9169, Joni & Friends, June 22, 2017, http://t.joniandfriends.org/radio/4-minute/god-permits-what/.

6. Joni Eareckson Tada, "Reflections on the 50th Anniversary of My Diving Accident," The Gospel Coalition, July 30, 2017, https://www.thegospelcoalition.org/article/reflections-on-50th-anniversary-of-my-diving-accident/.

7. Joni Eareckson Tada, "God Permits What He Hates," transcript of radio program #9169, Joni & Friends, January 31, 2014, https://old.joniandfriends.org/radio/4-minute/god-permits-what-he-hates2/.

8. Vance Christie, "'In Time of Trouble Say' (Andrew Murray)," VanceChristie.com, August 29, 2015, http://vancechristie.com/2015/08/29/in-time-of-trouble-say-andrew-murray/.

9. Ibid.

10. Warren W. Wiersbe, *Prayer, Praise and Promises: A Daily Walk through the Psalms* (Grand Rapids: Baker Books, 2011), 96.

11. Scotty Smith, *Every Season Prayers: Gospel-Centered Prayers for the Whole of Life* (Grand Rapids: Baker Books, 2016), 50. Note: the phrase *carpe diem* is Latin for "seize the day."

About the Authors

Robert and Nancy have been Mr. and Mrs. since 2015. Some of the story of their courtship and marriage is told in this book.

Even though they've each written twenty or more books, this is their first together. Robert is a gifted storyteller; Nancy loves to unpack sound biblical truth in a relatable way. Their hearts and voices have blended together in crafting this book.

Nancy founded and leads Revive Our Hearts, an international ministry that helps women experience freedom, fullness, and fruitfulness in Christ. Robert is the cofounder of Wolgemuth & Associates, a literary agency which represents the writing work of more than two hundred Christian authors.

Robert has two adult daughters, two sons-in-law, five grandchildren, and one grandson-in-law. Although she does not have biological offspring, Nancy's spiritual and relational children and grandchildren are legion. Robert discovered this when he married her.

Although they travel quite a bit, Nancy and Robert's favorite place to be is home in Michigan.

By Nancy DeMoss Wolgemuth

Adorned: Living Out the Beauty of the Gospel Together

Brokenness, Holiness, Surrender: A Revive Our Hearts Trilogy

Choosing Forgiveness: Your Journey to Freedom

Choosing Gratitude: Your Journey to Joy

The First Songs of Christmas: Meditations on Luke 1 & 2:
A 31-Day Advent Devotional

Lies Women Believe: And the Truth That Sets Them Free

Lies Young Women Believe: And the Truth That Sets Them Free
(coauthored with Dannah Gresh)

A Place of Quiet Rest: Finding Intimacy with God through a
Daily Devotional Life

The Quiet Place: Daily Devotional Readings

Seeking Him: Experiencing the Joy of Personal Revival
(coauthored with Tim Grissom)

True Woman 101: Divine Design: An 8-Week Study on Biblical
Womanhood (coauthored with Mary Kassian)

True Woman 201: Interior Design: 10 Elements of Biblical
Womanhood (coauthored with Mary Kassian)

The Wonder of His Name: 32 Life-Changing Names of Jesus

By Robert Wolgemuth

7 Things You Better Have Nailed Down before All Hell Breaks Loose

Couples of the Bible: A One-Year Devotional Study to Draw You Closer to God and Each Other (coauthored with Bobbie Wolgemuth)

The Father's Plan: A Bible Study for Dads

Lies Men Believe: And the Truth That Sets Them Free

Like the Shepherd: Leading Your Marriage with Love and Grace

Men of the Bible: A One-Year Devotional Study of Men in Scripture (coauthored with Ann Spangler)

The Most Important Place on Earth: What a Christian Home Looks Like and How to Build One

NIV Dad's Devotional Bible (notes)

She Calls Me Daddy: 7 Things You Need to Know about Building a Complete Daughter

She Still Calls Me Daddy: Building a New Relationship with Your Daughter after You Walk Her Down the Aisle

What Every Groom Needs to Know: The Most Important Year in a Man's Life (coauthored with Mark DeVries)

What's in the Bible: A One-Volume Guidebook to God's Word (coauthored with R.C. Sproul)